Praise for *Architecting for Scale*

Don't bet against your business. Build as if being successful at scale is a foregone conclusion. *Architecting for Scale* tells you in a no-nonsense way how to go about it.

—*Colin Bodell, VP Engineering, Shopify Plus; previously VP Website Applications Platform, Amazon.com*

Architecting for Scale is a definitive guide for directors, managers, and architects who want an actionable roadmap on operating at Scale.

—*Ken Gavranovic, EVP & GM New Relic; CEO/Founder (Interland, now web.com)*

Building systems with failure in mind is one of the keys to building highly scaled applications that perform. This book helps you learn this and other techniques to keep your applications performing as your customers—and your company—grow.

—*Patrick Franklin, EVP & CTO at American Express; previously VP of Engineering, Google*

This book helps show you how to keep your application performing while it— and your company—scale to meet your customer's growing needs.

—*Lew Cirne, CEO, New Relic*

SECOND EDITION

Architecting for Scale
*How to Maintain High Availability
and Manage Risk in the Cloud*

Lee Atchison

Beijing · Boston · Farnham · Sebastopol · Tokyo

Architecting for Scale

by Lee Atchison

Published by O'Reilly Media, Inc., 1005 Gravenstein Highway North, Sebastopol, CA 95472.

O'Reilly books may be purchased for educational, business, or sales promotional use. Online editions are also available for most titles (*http://oreilly.com*). For more information, contact our corporate/institutional sales department: 800-998-9938 or *corporate@oreilly.com*.

Acquisitions Editor: Kathleen Carr	**Indexer:** Ellen Troutman-Zaig
Developmental Editor: Amelia Blevins	**Interior Designer:** David Futato
Production Editor: Beth Kelly	**Cover Designer:** Karen Montgomery
Copyeditor: Jasmine Kwityn	**Illustrator:** Rebecca Demarest
Proofreader: Arthur Johnson	

July 2016:	First Edition
February 2020:	Second Edition

Revision History for the Second Edition

2020-02-28:   First Release

See *http://oreilly.com/catalog/errata.csp?isbn=9781492057178* for release details.

978-1-492-05717-8

[LSI]

To Beth

My love, my life, my everything

Table of Contents

Part II.   Tenet 2. Modern Application Architecture: Using Services

Part III.   Tenet 3. Organization: Scaling Your Organization for Modern Applications

Part IV.   Tenet 4. Risk: Risk Management for Modern Applications

Part V. Tenet 5. Cloud: Utilizing the Cloud

Forewords

Foreword for Second Edition

Architecting for Scale is a comprehensive book for managers who realize that all companies have shifted away from simply calling themselves "digital businesses" and instead now recognize that if they don't actually operate as one, they will go out of business. Banking, insurance, and other industries that used to have huge moats are being disrupted by upstart companies that deliver amazing experiences because they operate like a digital business rather than merely talking about being a digital business.

Architecting for Scale is a definitive guide for directors, managers, and architects who want an actionable roadmap on operating at scale with high reliability, implementing modern operational principles (DevOps, site reliability engineering), as well as how to use current state of the art concepts and services (microservices, cloud, edge).

I had the pleasure of working with Lee at New Relic, which enables companies to monitor their digital business across the globe. While at New Relic, Lee traveled around the world, helping companies navigate digital transformation, accelerate ideas into production, and deliver services that were up 100% of the time.

Time and time again, I have seen Lee leapfrog companies' transformation progress in a single thirty-minute meeting. Enjoy the book! It will be impactful to your company and your career!

— Ken Gavranovic
Former EVP & GM, New Relic
CEO/Founder, Interland (now Web.com)

Foreword for First Edition

We are living in interesting times, a software Cambrian explosion if you will, where the cost of building new systems has fallen by orders of magnitude and the connectivity of systems has grown by equal orders of magnitude. Resources like Amazon's AWS, Microsoft's Azure, and Google's GCP make it possible for us to physically scale our systems to sizes that we could only have imagined a few years ago.

The economics of these resources and seemingly limitless capacity is producing a uniquely rapid radiation of new ideas, new products, and new markets in ways that were never possible before. But all of these new explorations are possible only if the systems we build can scale. While it is easier than ever to build something small, building a system that can scale quickly and reliably proves to be a lot harder than just spinning up more hardware and more storage.

Software systems go through a predictable lifecycle starting with small well-crafted solutions fully understood by a single person, through the rapid growth into a monolith of technical debt, thence fissioning into an ad hoc collection of fragile services, and finally into a well-engineered distributed system able to scale reliably in both breadth (more users) and depth (more features). It's easy to see what needs to be done from the outside (make it more reliable!) and much harder to see the path from the inside. Fortunately, this book is the essential guidebook for the journey—from availability to service tiers, from game days to risk matrices, Lee describes the key decisions and practices for systems that scale.

Lee joined me at New Relic when we were first moving from being a single product monolith into being a multiproduct company, all while enjoying the hypergrowth in satisfied customers that made New Relic so successful. Lee came with a lot of experience at Amazon, both on the retail side, where they grew a lot, and on the AWS side, where—guess what?—they grew a lot. Lee has been part of teams and led teams and been actively involved in a whole lot of scaling, and he has the scars to prove it. Fortunately for us, he's lived through the mistakes and suffered through fiendishly difficult outages and is now passing along those lessons so that we don't have to get those same scars.

When Lee joined New Relic, we were suffering through our awkward teenage fail whale years. Our primitive monolith was suffering from our success, and our availability, reliability, and performance were not good. By putting in place the techniques he's written about in this book, we graduated from those high school years and built the robust enterprise-level service that exists today. One of our tools was establishing four levels of availability engineering: Bronze, Silver, Gold, and Platinum. To earn the Bronze level, a team had to have a risk matrix—it had to have defined SLAs. To earn the Silver level, a team had to be monitoring for the problems identified in the matrix and be using game days; Gold meant that the risks were mitigated; and Platinum was like a CMM Level 5 where the systems were self-healing and the focus was on continuous improvement. We prioritized these efforts for the Tier 1 services first, then the Tier 2 services, etc., and we eventually got everyone to at least Silver and most of the teams through Gold (and a couple to Platinum).

When I moved to InVision App, I joined a younger company, again moving through the transition from early success to hypergrowth, and thus I'm driving forward all these same techniques and tools that Lee describes. I urge you, in your journey as part of this exciting explosion of new systems and products and companies, to do the same: to learn from Lee in building your systems for scale.

— Bjorn Freeman-Benson, Ph.D.

Preface

Architecting for Scale is about modernization. It's about building and updating your critical applications to meet the needs of your increasingly demanding digital customers. It's about high availability, it's about architecting your applications using modern development and operations techniques, it's about organizing your development teams to help your applications—and your business—succeed, it's about scaling to your biggest days, it's about utilizing the resources available to you in the cloud to meet these challenges.

The process of architecting for scale is so much more than handling a large volume of traffic.

Who Should Read This Book

This book is intended for architects, managers, and directors who build and operate large-scale applications and systems, whether in an engineering or an operations organization. If you manage software developers, system reliability engineers, or operation teams, or you run an organization that contains large-scale applications and systems, the suggestions and guidance provided in this book will help you make your applications run smoother and more reliably.

If your application started small and has seen incredible growth (and is now experiencing some of the growing pains associated with that growth), you might be suffering from reduced reliability and reduced availability. If you struggle with managing technical debt and associated application failures, this book will provide guidance in reducing that technical debt to make your application able to handle larger scale more easily.

Why I Wrote This Book

After spending seven years working at Amazon building highly scaled applications in both the retail and the Amazon Web Services (AWS) worlds, I moved to New Relic, which was in the midst of hypergrowth. The company felt the pain of needing the systems and processes required to manage highly scaled applications, but it hadn't yet fully developed the processes and disciplines to scale its application.

At New Relic, I saw firsthand the struggles of a company going through the process of trying to scale, and I realized that there were many other companies experiencing the same struggles every day.

Now I travel all over the world, talking to customers and other people just like you about the cloud, about scaling, about availability, and about the critical process of building modern applications. I give presentations, panel discussions, classes, seminars. I talk one on one with engineering leaders and executives to both help them achieve their goals and learn from them what works and what doesn't work. I write articles. I give interviews. I participate in podcasts.

My intent with this book is to help others working with high-growth applications to learn processes and best practices that can assist them in avoiding the pitfalls awaiting them as they scale.

Whether your application is growing tenfold or just 10% each year, and whether the growth is in number of users, number of transactions, amount of data stored, or code complexity, this book can help you build and maintain your application to handle that growth, while maintaining a high level of availability.

A Word on Scale Today

As applications grow, two things begin to happen: they become significantly more complicated, and they handle significantly larger traffic volumes.

Increased complexity means increased brittleness. More traffic means more novel and complex mechanisms to manage the traffic.

Application developers seldom build scalability into their applications from the beginning. We often think we have built in scalability, and we believe we've done what was necessary to let our application scale to the highest levels we can imagine. But more often than not, we find faults in our logic and in our applications. These faults appear only after we begin to see scaling problems, and that makes scaling to larger traffic volumes and larger datasets more difficult.

This leads to even greater complexity and even more brittleness.

Ultimately, this scale/brittleness/scale/complexity cycle turns into a death spiral for an application, as it experiences brownouts, blackouts, and other quality-of-service and availability problems.

But these are *your* problems. Your customers don't care about these issues. They just want to use your application to do the job they expect it to do. If your application is down, slow, or inconsistent, customers will simply abandon it and seek out competitors that can handle their business.

How can we improve the scalability of our applications, even when we begin to reach these limits? Obviously, the sooner we consider scalability in the lifecycle of an application, the easier it will be to scale. Yet we don't want to overarchitect our applications for scalability beyond what is required. At any point during the lifecycle, there are many techniques you can use to improve the scalability of your application.

But before you can consider techniques for scaling your application, you must get your application availability in shape. Nothing else matters until you make this leap and make these improvements. If you do not implement these changes now, up front, you will find that as your application scales, you will begin to lose sight of how it's working, and random, unexpected problems will begin occurring. These problems will create outages and data loss and will significantly affect your ability to build and improve your application. Furthermore, as traffic and data increases, these problems simply become worse. Before doing anything else, get your availability and risk management in order.

What's New in the Second Edition

While many of the concepts discussed in this book are mostly timeless, many (such as serverless computing) have had to be updated to reflect industry changes over the last four years.

Additionally, I've spent the last several years traveling around the world talking and speaking about these topics. I've learned a lot from various interactions with customers and other experts, and I've incorporated much of what I've learned into this edition.

An extensive update on cloud utilization has also been added to this book.

Finally, the content has been significantly restructured and reorganized from the first edition to make the information more accessible and relevant.

Using the Cloud

Cloud-based services are growing and expanding at extremely high speeds. Software as a Service (SaaS) is becoming the norm for application development, primarily because of the need for providing these cloud-based services. SaaS applications are particularly sensitive to scaling issues due to their multi-tenant nature.

As our world changes and we focus more and more on SaaS services, cloud-based services, and high-volume applications, scaling becomes increasingly important.

There does not seem to be an end in sight to the size and complexity to which our cloud applications can grow.

The very mechanisms that are state of the art today for managing scale will be nothing more than basic tenants tomorrow, and the solutions to tomorrow's scaling issues will make today's solutions look simplistic and minimalistic. Our industry will demand more and more complex systems and architectures to handle the scale of tomorrow.

Naturally, as time goes on, some material in this book will become dated. My intent is to provide as much content as possible that stands the test of time.

Services Versus Microservices

There is much controversy in the industry about use of the terms *service* and *microservice*. I personally do not like the term *microservice* because it implies a specific sizing of a service that is not necessarily a healthy assumption. Many services are small, and some are truly "micro," but many are much larger too. The appropriate size determination is based on context and is subject to many concerns and criteria,[1] and in my mind the use of the term *microservices* biases this discussion. However, I recognize that the term *microservice* has gained strong popularity in the industry.

There are also people that pigeonhole use of the term *service* as part of the term *SOA* and further pigeonhole these terms to refer to a particular type of architecture offering that was popular a decade or more ago. I find these comparisons inaccurate and confusing.

My personal preference is to use the term *service*, but I recognize many people use the term *microservice*. So I tend to use both terms in my discussions with other companies, depending on context. *In my mind, both terms mean the exact same thing.*

There is another use of the word *service*, though, that is worth discussing. This is when you refer to an external service, such as when you say "Amazon offers the Amazon S3 *service*." This use of the word *service* is *seemingly* distinct, and *seems* like a different use of the word *service*, but in reality it is the same thing. A "service" is a software module that provides a very specific piece of functionality and the data that supports that functionality. Whether the service is written by your developers or by engineers over at Amazon is irrelevant. I do recognize that sometimes it is important to distinguish between these two types of services, however.

So this is how I will use these terms in this book. I'll use both terms interchangeably, depending on context. You will definitely see my bias toward the word *service* in this

---

1 I talk about service sizing in greater detail in "Dividing into Services" on page 44.

book. *You should assume both terms mean the exact same thing.* When I am referring to a specific type of service provided by another company, such as a cloud service, I will so indicate. In these cases, you will see the use of terms such as "AWS service" or "cloud service" or "SaaS service."

Modern Digital Customer Experiences

In our modern digital world, software applications become the face of our brand and our company. The way our customers interact with us is through our software. Our applications aren't just part of the customer experience. In many cases, they are the *entire* customer experience. Software is critical to our success, and modern customers expect our applications to also be modern. How our customers perceive our brands and our company depends greatly on how they perceive our software.

A Non-Modern Application

Consider this example: my son has an application on his smartphone that he has to use to get some of his medical benefits. It is a government application, built and run by the US government.

This application doesn't work all the time. When you launch the application at an odd time of day, you get an error message. The error message says, "This application is only available to use between the hours of 9–5, Monday–Friday, Eastern Time."

Yep, that's right. This is a mobile software application on his smartphone, and the software is disabled except during East Coast business hours.

Can your business operate with an application such as this? Can it operate with this type of restriction on its use? Can any commercial business put limits like this on its customers and stay in business?

No, I bet there isn't a single commercial enterprise out there that can survive and treat its customers this way. Instead, we have to provide our customers with memorable customer experiences. Our applications must work whenever our customers want to use them. Everything needs to work 100% of the time, 24 hours a day, 7 days a week. If not, we disappoint our customers, and disappointed customers go away.

Navigating This Book

Managing scale is not only about managing traffic volume—it also involves managing risk and availability. Often, all these things are different ways of describing the same problem, and they all go hand in hand. Thus, to properly discuss scale, we must also consider availability, risk management, team/organization processes, and modern architecture paradigms such as microservices and cloud computing.

As such, this book is organized into five major parts, each representing a major tenet of architecting for scale. Let's take a look at each of these.

Tenet 1. Availability: Maintaining Availability in Modern Applications

Modern software must maintain a high level of availability. Customers will not tolerate outages. If your application does not function when your customer needs it, they will not remain a customer for long.

Part I discusses the importance of application availability to our customers, and how it is impacted by application scaling. Understanding, measuring, and improving availability are the focus of these chapters.

Chapters in this part include:

- Chapter 1, *Understanding, Measuring, and Improving Your Availability*
- Chapter 2, *Two Mistakes High—Having Room to Recover from Mistakes*

Tenet 2. Modern Application Architecture: Using Services

Modern software requires the use of modern application architectures. Modern application architectures require moving away from monolithic applications and embracing service-based architectures.

Monolith applications are extremely hard to scale, both from a traffic scaling standpoint and from the standpoint of your ability to scale the size of your organization to work on the application. The larger the monolith, the slower it is to make changes to the application, the fewer the people who can work on it and manage it effectively, and the greater the likelihood that traffic variations and growth will negatively impact availability.

Service-oriented architectures solve these problems by providing greater flexibility in scaling based on traffic needs. In addition, they provide a scalable framework to allow larger development organizations to work on the application, allowing the applications themselves to get larger and more complex.

Chapters in Part II include:

- Chapter 3, *Using Services*
- Chapter 4, *Services and Data*
- Chapter 5, *Dealing with Service Failures*

Tenet 3. Organization: Scaling Your Organization for Modern Applications

You cannot build modern software unless your development organization makes use of modern processes and procedures. This includes service ownership responsibilities and development processes.

It doesn't matter how scalable your application is; you cannot scale your application if your development organization isn't structured to support it, or if your organization does not have the right culture to drive higher availability and greater scalability.

Organizing your teams to better support your scalability needs will create a culture that supports your application's scaling needs.

Chapters in Part III include:

- Chapter 6, *Service Ownership—STOSA*
- Chapter 7, *Service Tiers*
- Chapter 8, *Service-Level Agreements*

Tenet 4. Risk: Risk Management for Modern Applications

You cannot remove all risk from a system. It just isn't possible. All complex systems have inherent risk. Instead, we must learn to manage the risk and use risk as a tool for evaluating technical debt and making decisions on application improvements.

Understanding risk, measuring risk, and prioritizing activities based on measured risk are important tools for building highly scaled, high-availability applications.

Chapters in Part IV include:

- Chapter 9, *Using Risk Management When Architecting for Scale*
- Chapter 10, *Game Days*
- Chapter 11, *Building Systems with Reduced Risk*

Tenet 5. Cloud: Utilizing the Cloud

High availability in a modern application requires nimble scaling. We can no longer afford to have excess infrastructure capacity lying around to meet the peak needs of our application. Instead, we must dynamically allocate and consume infrastructure resources, on demand, based on our current needs.

Dynamic infrastructures, and applications that can support and optimize dynamic infrastructures, are a critical architectural component to building highly scaled, highly available applications.

Dynamic infrastructures are the cornerstone benefit of the public cloud. Utilizing the public cloud is essential to keeping your application highly available at scale.

Chapters in Part V include:

- Chapter 12, *Getting Started Architecting for Scale with the Cloud*
- Chapter 13, *Five Industry Trends Changed by the Cloud*
- Chapter 14, *Types of SaaS and Tenancy*
- Chapter 15, *Distributing Your Application in the AWS Cloud*
- Chapter 16, *Managed Infrastructure*
- Chapter 17, *Cloud Resource Allocation*
- Chapter 18, *Serverless and Functions as a Service*
- Chapter 19, *Edge Computing*
- Chapter 20, *Geographic Impact on Using the Cloud*

These are the five critical tenets to building applications that meet the modern needs of our customers. These tenets form the basis of *Architecting for Scale*.

Online Resources

The *Architecting for Scale* website (*www.architectingforscale.com*) offers additional information about this book, including links to supplementary material. You can find more information about me on my website at *www.leeatchison.com*, and you can also follow my blog at *www.leeatscale.com*.

Conventions Used in This Book

The following typographical conventions are used in this book:

 This element signifies a tip or suggestion.

This element signifies a general note.

O'Reilly Online Learning

 For more than 40 years, *O'Reilly Media* has provided technology and business training, knowledge, and insight to help companies succeed.

Our unique network of experts and innovators share their knowledge and expertise through books, articles, conferences, and our online learning platform. O'Reilly's online learning platform gives you on-demand access to live training courses, in-depth learning paths, interactive coding environments, and a vast collection of text and video from O'Reilly and 200+ other publishers. For more information, please visit *http://oreilly.com*.

How to Contact Us

Please address comments and questions concerning this book to the publisher:

O'Reilly Media, Inc.
1005 Gravenstein Highway North
Sebastopol, CA 95472
800-998-9938 (in the United States or Canada)
707-829-0515 (international or local)
707-829-0104 (fax)

We have a web page for this book, where we list errata, examples, and any additional information. You can access this page at *https://oreil.ly/architecting-for-scale-2e*.

Email *bookquestions@oreilly.com* to comment or ask technical questions about this book.

For more information about our books, courses, conferences, and news, see our website at *http://www.oreilly.com*.

Find us on Facebook: *http://facebook.com/oreilly*

Follow us on Twitter: *http://twitter.com/oreillymedia*

Watch us on YouTube: *http://www.youtube.com/oreillymedia*

Acknowledgments

While there are more people who helped make this book possible than I could possibly ever list here, I do want to mention several people who were particularly helpful to me:

- Ken Gavranovic, the word *friend* is not sufficient to describe you. Always trust the power of monkeys.

- Bjorn Freeman-Benson, who supported me significantly in the early stages of developing the first edition of this book, and who gave me opportunities at New Relic that helped provide me the insights I needed for this book. I am so glad our friendship has continued past those days we directly worked together.

- Kevin McGuire, who has been a friend and confidant. We started at New Relic together, and it was your foresight and imagination that has helped give my career the needed focus and direction that guides me today.

- Abner Germanow, Darren Cunningham, Jay Fry, Bharath Gowda, and Robson Grieve, who took a chance on me and fought to get me my thought leadership role at New Relic. The days I worked with you all were by far the most fun, rewarding, and personally fulfilling I have ever had. I miss those times greatly. Abner in particular, without you I would not have the career I have today. You guided me into this new role and helped me grow from an engineer and architect into a strategist, pundit, and thought leader. Thank you for believing in me and mentoring me along that path.

- Jim Gochee, who introduced me to the magic that was New Relic, both as a product and eventually as a career.

- Lew Cirne, whose vision has given us New Relic, and me a career and a home. The joy and driven enthusiasm you get after meeting with Lew one on one is highly infectious and hugely empowering. No wonder New Relic is so successful.

- Kevin Downs, my friend and cloud buddy. Say hi to the mouse for me. Oh, and by the way, containers rule.

- Brandon SanGiovanni, my friend. From MLB to Marvel and Mickey, you've dealt firsthand with many of the challenges I discuss in this book, and you are still alive and smiling! Thank you for your support, your knowledge, and, most importantly, your friendship.

- Abbas Haider Ali, who is someone I greatly respect. We both have roles as industry thought leaders, and it's great to have someone to bounce ideas off of and get suggestions from. Your input in early drafts of this book has made it substantially better. Thank you!

- Kurt Kufeld, who mentored me and helped me fit into the weird, chaotic, challenging, draining, and ultimately hugely rewarding world called Amazon.

- Greg Hart, Scott Green, Patrick Franklin, Suresh Kumar, Colin Bodell, and Andy Jassy, who gave me opportunities at Amazon and AWS I could not have ever imagined.

- Brian Anderson, my original editor, and Kathleen Carr, my current editor at O'Reilly. Together, they are responsible for making this book and many other projects at O'Reilly Media happen. Brian made the first edition of this book possible. Kathleen encouraged and enabled me to build the much expanded second edition, along with several courses, trainings, and knowledge sessions.

- Amelia Blevins from O'Reilly, who made substantial editorial suggestions to the format, layout, and content of this expanded second edition of the book. These suggestions made a huge difference in the quality and readability of the book. If you like the new structure of this second edition, you have Amelia to thank for it.

To all of those people who reached out to me after reading the first edition of this book, giving me your praise, encouragement, and suggestions, I thank you for helping to keep me motivated and to give me ideas for the improvements that went into this second edition.

To my family, and especially my wife, Beth, who is my constant light and guide through this life we have together. My days are brighter, and my path is clearer, because she is with me.

To all these people, and all the people I did not mention, my heartfelt thank you.

I can't end without also mentioning the furry ones: Issie, the snoring spaniel, and Abbey, the joyful corgi. And finally, Budha, the krazy kitty, who contributed more than his share of typos to this book.

Tenet 1. Availability: Maintaining Availability in Modern Applications

Without high availability, you have no reason to scale.

Modern software must maintain a high level of availability. Customers will not tolerate outages. If your application does not function when your customer needs it, they will not remain a customer for long.

Application availability is incredibly important to us and our customers, and it impacts how we think about application scalability. Understanding, measuring, and improving availability are the focus of the chapters in this part.

CHAPTER 1

Understanding, Measuring, and Improving Your Availability

The Big Game

It's Sunday—the day of the big game. You've invited 20 of your closest friends over to watch the game on your new 300-inch Ultra Max TV. Everyone has come, and your house is full of snacks and beer. Everyone is laughing. The game is about to start. And...

...the lights go out...

...the TV goes dark...

...the game, for you and your friends, is over.

Disappointed, you pick up the phone and call the local power company. The representative, unsympathetically, says: "We're sorry, but we guarantee only 95% availability of our power grid."

Why is availability important? Because your customers expect your service to work... all the time. Anything less than 100% availability can be catastrophic to your business.

No one cares whether your system has great features if they can't use it.

One of the most important topics in architecting for scalable systems is availability. Although there are some companies and some services for which a certain amount of downtime is reasonable and expected, most businesses cannot have any downtime at all without it affecting their customers' satisfaction, and ultimately the company's bottom line.

The following are fundamental questions that all companies must ask as they determine how important system availability is to themselves and their customers. It is these questions, and the inevitable answers to them, that are the core of why availability is critical to highly scaled applications.

Why buy from you?
> Why should someone buy your service if it is not operational when they need it?

What do your customers think?
> What do your customers think or feel when they need to use your service and it's not operational?

How do you make customers happy?
> How can you make your customers happy, make your company money, and meet your business promises and requirements if your service is down?

> Keeping your customers happy and engaged with your system is possible only if your system is operational. There is a direct and meaningful correlation between system availability and customer satisfaction.

High availability is such a critical component of building highly scalable systems that we will devote a significant amount of time to the topic in this book. How do you build a system (a service or application or environment) that is highly available even when a wide range of demands are placed on it?

Availability Versus Reliability

Availability and reliability are two similar yet very different concepts. It is important to understand the difference between them.

Reliability, in our context, generally refers to the quality of a system. Typically, it means the ability of a system to consistently perform according to specifications. You speak of software as reliable if it passes its test suites and does generally what you think it should do. Reliability answers the question:

> "Is the response to my query correct?"

Availability, in our context, generally refers to the ability of your system to perform the tasks it is capable of doing. Is the system around? Is it operational? Is it responding? If the answer is "yes," it is available. Availability answers the questions:

> "Am I getting a response?"
> "Did the response arrive in time?"

As you can see, availability and reliability are very similar. It is hard for a system to be available if it is not also reliable, and it is hard for a system to be reliable if it is not also available.

More formally, here is what we mean when we use these terms:

Reliability
> The ability of your system to perform the operations it is intended to perform without making a mistake.

Availability
> The ability of your system to be operational when needed in order to perform those operations.

A system that adds 2 + 3 and gets 6 has poor reliability. A system that adds 2 + 3 and never returns a result at all has poor availability. Reliability can often be fixed by testing. Availability is usually much harder to solve.

You can introduce a software bug in your application that can cause 2 + 3 to produce the answer 6. This can be easily caught and fixed in a test suite.

However, assume you have an application that reliably produces the result 2 + 3 = 5. Now imagine running this application on a computer that has a flaky network connection. The result? You run the application, and sometimes it returns 5, and sometimes it doesn't return anything. The application may be reliable, but it is not available.

We will focus almost exclusively on architecting highly available systems. We will assume your system is reliable, we will assume you know how to build and run test suites, and we will discuss reliability only when it has a direct impact on your system architecture or its availability.

What Causes Poor Availability?

What causes an application that previously performed well to begin exhibiting poor availability? There are many possible causes:

Resource exhaustion
> Increase the number of users or increase the amount of data in use in a system and your application may fall victim to resource exhaustion, resulting in a slower and unresponsive application.

Unplanned load-based changes
> Increases in the popularity of your application might require code and application changes to handle the increased load. These changes, often implemented quickly and at the last minute with little or no forethought or planning, increase the likelihood of problems occurring.

Increased number of moving parts
> As an application gains popularity, it is often necessary to assign more and more developers, designers, testers, and other individuals to work on and maintain it.

This larger number of individuals working on the application creates a large number of moving parts, whether those moving parts are new features, changed features, or just general application maintenance. The more individuals working on the application, the more moving parts within the application and the greater the chance for bad interactions to occur in it.

Outside dependencies

The more dependencies your application has on external resources, such as SaaS services, infrastructure, or cloud-based services, the more it is exposed to availability problems caused by those resources.

Technical debt

Increases in the applications complexity typically increase technical debt (i.e., the accumulation of desired software changes and pending bug fixes that often build up over time as an application grows and matures). Technical debt increases the likelihood of a problem occurring.

All fast-growing applications have one, some, or all of these problems. As such, potential availability problems can begin occurring in applications that previously performed flawlessly. The problems can quietly creep up on you, or the problems may start suddenly without warning.

But most growing applications will eventually begin having availability problems.

Availability problems cost you money, they cost your customers money, and they cost you your customers' trust and loyalty. Your company cannot survive for long if you constantly have availability problems.

Building applications designed to scale means building applications designed for high availability.

Measuring Availability

Measuring availability is important to keeping your system highly available. Only by measuring availability can you understand how your application is performing now and examine how your application's availability changes over time.

The most widely held mechanism for measuring the availability of a web application is calculating the percent of time it's accessible for use by customers. We can describe this by using the following formula for a given period:

Site availability percentage = total_seconds_in_period − seconds_system_is_down / total_seconds_in_period

Let's consider an example. Suppose that over the month of April, your website was down twice; the first time it was down for 37 minutes, and the second time it was down for 15 minutes. What is the availability of your website?

You can see from the following example that it takes only a small amount of outage to have an impact on your availability percentage:

Total number of seconds down = (37 + 15) × 60 = 3,120 s

Total number of seconds in month = 30 days × 86,400 s/day = 2,592,000 s

Site availability percentage = total_seconds_in_period − seconds_system_is_down / total_seconds_in_period

Site availability percentage = 2,592,000 s − 3,120 s / 2,592,000 s

Site availability percentage = 99.8795

Your site availability is 99.8795%.

The Nines

Often you will hear availability described as "the nines." This is a shorthand way of indicating high-availability percentages. Table 1-1 illustrates what it means. An application that has "2 nines" availability must be available 99% of the time. This means in a typical month it can be down for 432 minutes and still meet the 99% available goal. By contrast, a "4 nines" application must be available 99.99% of the time, meaning it can be down a mere four minutes in a typical month.

Table 1-1. The nines

Nines	Percentage	Monthly outage
2 nines	99%	432 minutes
3 nines	99.9%	43 minutes
4 nines	99.99%	4 minutes
5 nines	99.999%	26 seconds
6 nines	99.9999%	2.6 seconds

In the preceding example, we see that the website has fallen just short of the 3 nines metric (99.8795% compared to 99.9%). For a website that maintains 5 nines of availability, there can be only 26 *seconds* of downtime every *month*.

What's a reasonable availability number in order to consider your system as high availability? It is impossible to give a single answer to this question because it depends dramatically on your website, your customer expectations, your business needs, and your business expectations. You need to determine for yourself what number is required for your business.

Often, for basic web applications, 3 nines is considered *acceptable availability*. Using Table 1-1, this amounts to 43 minutes of downtime every month.

Planned Outages Are Still Outages

Don't be fooled into thinking your site is highly available when it isn't. Planned and regular maintenance that involves your application being unavailable still count against availability.

Here's a comment that I often overhear: "Our application never fails. That's because we regularly perform system maintenance. By scheduling weekly two-hour maintenance windows and performing maintenance during these windows, we keep our availability high."

Does this group keep its application's availability high?

Let's find out:

> Site availability percentage = total_hours_in_period − hours_system_is_down / total_hours_in_period
>
> hours_in_week = 7 days × 24 hours = 168 hours
>
> hours_unavailable_each_week = 2 hours
>
> Site availability (no failures) = 168 hours − 2 hours / 168 hours = 98.8%
>
> Site availability (no failures) = 98.8%

Without having a single failure of its application, the best this organization can achieve is 98.8% availability. This falls short of even 2 nines availability (98.8% versus 99%).

Planned maintenance hurts nearly as much as unplanned outages. If your customer needs your application to be available and it isn't, your customer has a negative experience. It doesn't matter whether or not you planned for the outage.

Availability by the Numbers

Measuring availability is important to keeping your system highly available, now and in the future. This section discussed a common mechanism for measuring availability and provided some guidelines for what is considered reasonable availability.

Improving Your Availability When It Slips

Your application is operational and online. Your systems are in place, and your team is operating efficiently. Everything seems to be going well. Your traffic is steadily increasing, and your sales organization is very happy. All is well.

Then there's a bit of a slip. Your system suffers an unanticipated outage. But that's OK; your availability has been fantastic until now. A little outage is no big deal. Your traffic is still increasing. Everyone shrugs it off—it was just "one of those things."

Then it happens again—another outage. Oops. Well, OK. Overall, we're still doing well. No need to panic; it was just another "one of those things."

Then another outage...

Now your CEO is a bit concerned. Customers are beginning to ask what's going on. Your sales team is starting to worry.

Then another outage...

Suddenly, your once stable and operational system is becoming less and less stable; your outages are getting more and more attention.

Now you've got real problems.

What happened? Keeping your system highly available is a daunting task. What do you do if availability begins to slip? What do you do if your application availability has fallen or begins to fall, and you need to improve it to keep your customers satisfied?

Knowing what you can do when your availability begins to slip will help you to avoid falling into a vicious cycle of problems. What can you do to avoid your availability slipping? Some key things are:

- Measure and track your current availability
- Automate your manual processes
- Automate your deployment processes
- Maintain and track all configurations in a management system
- Allow quick changes and experiments, with an easy rollback capability if a problem occurs
- Aim to continuously improve your applications and systems
- Keep on top of availability as a core issue as your application changes and grows

The following sections detail these key steps in further detail.

Measure and Track Your Current Availability

To understand what is happening to your availability, you must first measure what your current availability is. Tracking when your application is or is not available gives you an availability percentage that can show how you are performing over a specific period of time. You can use this to determine whether your availability is improving or faltering.

You should continuously monitor your availability percentage and report the results on a regular basis. On top of this, overlay key events in your application, such as when you performed system changes and improvements. This way you can see whether there is a correlation over time between system events and availability issues. This can help you to identify risks to your availability.

Next, you must understand how your application can be expected to perform from an availability standpoint. A tool that you can use to help manage your application availability is service tiers. These are simply labels associated with services that indicate how critical a service is to the operation of your business. The use of service tiers allows you and your teams to distinguish between mission-critical services and those that are valuable but not essential. We'll discuss service tiers in more depth in Chapter 7.

Finally, create and maintain a *risk matrix*. With this tool, you can gain visibility into the technical debt and associated risk present in your application. Risk matrices are covered more fully in Chapter 9.

Now that you have a way to track your availability and a way of identifying and managing your risk, you will want to review your risk management plans on a regular basis.

Additionally, you should create and implement mitigation plans to reduce your application risks. This will give you a concrete set of tasks you and your development teams can implement to tackle the riskiest parts of your application. This is discussed in detail in Chapter 9.

Automate Your Manual Processes

To maintain high availability, you need to remove unknowns and variables. Performing manual operations is a common way to insert variable results and/or unknown results into your system.

You should never perform a manual operation on a production system.

When you make a change to your system, the change might improve your system, or it might compromise it. Using only repeatable tasks gives you the following:

- The ability to test a task before implementing it. Testing what happens when you make a specific change is critical to avoiding mistakes that cause outages.
- The ability to tweak the task to perform exactly what you want it to do. This lets you implement improvements to the change you are about to make before you actually make the change.
- The ability to have the task reviewed by a third party. This increases the likelihood that the task will have no unexpected side effects.
- The ability to put the task under version control. Version control systems allow you to determine when the task is changed, by whom, and for what reasons.

- The ability to apply the task to related resources. Making a change to a single server that improves how that server works is great. Being able to apply the same change to every affected server in a consistent way makes the task even more useful.

- The ability to have all related resources act consistently. If you continuously make "one-off" changes to resources such as servers, the servers will begin to drift and act differently from one another. This makes it difficult to diagnose problematic servers because there will be no baseline of operational expectation that you can use for comparison.

- The ability to implement repeatable tasks. Repeatable tasks are auditable tasks. Auditable tasks are tasks that you can analyze later for their impact, positive or negative, on the system as a whole.

There are many systems for which no one has access to the production environment. Period. The only access to production is through automated processes and procedures. The owners of these systems lock down their environments like this specifically for the aforementioned reasons.

In summary, if you can't repeat a task, it isn't a useful task. There are many places where adding repeatability to changes will help keep your system and application stable. This includes implementing server configuration changes, making performance-tuning tweaks and adjustments, restarting servers, restarting jobs and tasks, changing routing rules, and upgrading and deploying software packages. We'll now look at some examples of repeatable tasks you should employ.

Automated deploys

By automating deploys, you guarantee that changes are applied consistently throughout your system, and that you can apply similar changes later with known results. Additionally, rollbacks to known good states become more reliable with automated deployment systems.

Configuration management

Rather than "tweaking a configuration variable" in the kernel of a server, use a process to apply the change in an automated manner.

At the very least, write a script that will make the change, and then check that script into your software change management system. This enables you to make the same change to all servers in your system uniformly. Additionally, when you need to add a new server to your system or replace an old one, having a known configuration that can be applied improves the likelihood that you can add the new server to your system safely, with minimal impact.

But even better—and consistent with modern, state of the art, configuration management best practices—is to employ a concept called Infrastructure as Code. Infrastructure as Code involves describing your infrastructure in a standard, machine-readable specification and then passing that specification through an infrastructure tool that will create and/or update your infrastructure and your configuration to match the specification. Tools like Puppet and Chef can help make this process easier to manage.

Then you take this specification and check it into your version control system, so that changes to the specification can be tracked just like code changes can be tracked. Running the specification through the infrastructure tool anytime a change is made to the specification will update your live infrastructure to match the specification.

If anyone needs to make a change to the infrastructure or its configuration, they must make the change to the specification, check the change into version control, and then "deploy" the change via the infrastructure tool to update your live infrastructure to match. In this manner, you can:

1. Ensure all components of the infrastructure have a consistent, known, and stable configuration.
2. Track all changes to the infrastructure so they can be rolled back if needed, or used to assist in correlation with system events and outages.
3. Allow a peer review process, similar to a code review process, to ensure changes to your infrastructure are correct and appropriate.
4. Allow creating duplicate environments to assist in testing, staging, and development with an environment identical to production.

This same sort of process applies to all infrastructure components. This includes not only servers and their operating system configuration but also other cloud components, VPCs, load balancers, switches, routers, network components, and monitoring applications and systems.

For Infrastructure as Code management to be useful, it must be employed for all system changes, all the time. It is never acceptable to bypass the infrastructure management system to make a change, no matter the circumstances. Not ever.

You would be surprised the number of times I have received an operational update email that said something like, "We had a problem with one of our servers last night. We hit a limit to the maximum number of open files the server could handle. So I tweaked the kernel variable and increased the maximum number of open files, and the server is operational again."

That is, it is operating correctly until someone accidentally overwrites the change because there was no documentation of the change. Or until one of the other servers running the application has the same problem but did not have this change applied to it.

Or someone makes another change, which breaks the application because it is inconsistent with the undocumented change you just made.

Consistency, repeatability, and unfaltering attention to detail are critical to making a configuration management process work. And a standard and repeatable configuration management process such as we describe here is critical to keeping your scaled system highly available.

Change experiments and high frequency changes

Another advantage of having a highly repeatable, highly automated process for making changes and upgrades to your system is that it allows you to experiment with changes. Suppose that you have a configuration change you want to make to your servers that you believe will improve their performance in your application. By using an automated change management process, you can do the following:

- Document your proposed change.
- Review the change with people who are knowledgeable and might be able to provide suggestions and improvements.
- Test the change on servers in a test or staging environment.
- Deploy your change quickly and easily.
- Examine the results quickly. If the change didn't have the desired results, you can quickly roll back to a known good state.

The keys to implementing this process are to have an automated change process with rollback capabilities, and to have the ability to make small changes to your system easily and often.[1] The former lets you make changes consistently; the latter lets you experiment and roll back failed experiments with little to no impact on your customers.

Automated change sanity testing

By having an automated change and deploy process,[2] you can implement an automated sanity test of all changes. You can use a browser testing application for web

---

1 According to Werner Vogels, CTO of Amazon, in 2014 Amazon did 50 million deploys to individual hosts. That's about one every second.

2 This could be, but does not need to be, a modern continuous integration and continuous deploy (CI/CD) process.

applications or use a synthetic monitoring system to simulate customer interaction with your application.

When you are ready to deploy a change to production, you can have your deployment system first automatically deploy the change to a test or staging environment. You can then have these automated tests run and validate that the changes did not break your application.

If and when those tests pass, you can automatically deploy the change in a consistent manner to your production environment. Depending on how your tests are constructed, you should be able to run the tests regularly on your production environment as well to validate that no changes break anything there.

By automating the entire process, you can increase your confidence that a change will not have a negative impact on your production systems.

Improve Your Systems

Now that you have a system to monitor availability, a way to track risk and mitigations in your system, and a way to easily and safely apply consistent changes to your system, you can focus your efforts on improving the availability of your application itself.

Regularly review your risk matrix and your recovery plans. Make reviewing them part of your postmortem process. Execute projects that are designed to mitigate the risks identified in your matrix. Roll out those changes in an automated and safe way, using the sanity tests discussed earlier. Examine how the mitigation has improved your availability. Continue the process until your availability reaches the level you want and need it to be.

Keep on Top of Availability in Your Changing and Growing Application

As your system grows, you'll need to handle larger and larger traffic and data demands. Much of the content in this book is designed to help you address application availability and scalability issues as your application grows and changes. In particular, managing mistakes and errors at scale is discussed in Chapter 2. Service tiers, which you can use to identify key availability-impacting services, are discussed in Chapter 7. And service-level agreement (SLA) management is discussed in Chapter 8.

Typically, your application will change continuously. As such, your risks, mitigations, contingencies, and recovery plans need to constantly change.

Knowing what you can do when your availability begins to slip will help you to avoid falling into a vicious cycle of problems.

Five Focuses to Improve Application Availability

Building a scalable application that has high availability is not easy and does not come automatically. Problems can crop up in unexpected ways that can cause your beautifully functioning application to stop working for all or some of your customers.

These availability problems often arise from the areas you least expect, and some of the most serious availability problems can originate from extremely benign sources.

A Simple Icon Failure

A classic example of the pitfalls of ignoring dependency failure occurred in a real-life application I worked on. The application provided a service to customers, and on the top of every page was a customizable icon representing the currently logged-in user. The icon was generated by a third-party system.

One day, the third-party system that generated the icon failed. Our application, which assumed that system would always work, didn't know what to do. As a result, our application failed as well. Our entire application failed simply because the icon generation system—a very minor "feature"—failed.

How could we have avoided this problem? If we had simply anticipated that the third-party system might fail, we would have walked through this failure scenario during design and discovered that our application would fail subsequently. We could then have added logic to detect the failure and remove the icon if the failure occurred, or simply catch the error when it occurred and not allowed it to propagate down and affect the working aspects of the page.

A simple check and some error recovery logic would have kept the application operational. Instead, our application experienced a major site outage.

All because of the lack of an icon.

No one can anticipate where problems will come from, and no amount of testing will find all issues. Many of these are systemic problems, not merely code problems.

To find these availability problems, we need to step back and take a systemic look at your application and how it works. Here are five things you can and should focus on when building a system to make sure that, as its use scales upwards, availability remains high:

- Build with failure in mind
- Always think about scaling
- Mitigate risk

- Monitor availability
- Respond to availability issues in a predictable and defined way

Let's look at each of these individually.

Focus #1: Build with Failure in Mind

As Werner Vogels, CTO of Amazon, says, "Everything fails all the time." Plan on your applications and services failing. It will happen. Now, deal with it.

Assuming your application will fail, how will it fail? As you build your system, consider availability concerns during all aspects of your system design and construction.

Design

What design constructs and patterns have you considered or are you using that will help improve the availability of your software?

Using design constructs and patterns, such as simple error catching deep within your application, retry logic, and circuit breakers, allows you to catch errors when they have affected the smallest available subset of functionality. This allows you to limit the scope of a problem and have your application still provide useful capabilities even if part of the application is failing.

Dependencies

What do you do when a component you depend on fails? How do you retry? What do you do if the problem is an unrecoverable (hard) failure, rather than a recoverable (soft) failure?

Circuit breaker patterns are particularly useful for handling dependency failures because they can reduce the impact a dependency failure has on your system. Without a circuit breaker, you can decrease the performance of your application because of a dependency failure (e.g., because an unacceptably long timeout is required to detect the failure). With a circuit breaker, you can "give up" and stop using a dependency until you are certain that dependency has recovered.

Customers

What do you do when a component that is a customer of your system behaves poorly? Can you handle excessive load on your system? Can you throttle excessive traffic? Can you handle garbage data passed in? What about excessive data?

Sometimes denial-of-service attacks can come from "friendly" sources. For example, a customer of your application may see a sudden surge in activity that requires a significant increase in the volume of requests to your application. Alternatively, a bug in your customer's application may cause them to call your application at an unacceptably high rate. What do you do when this happens? Does the sudden increase in traffic bring your application down? Or can you detect this problem and throttle the request rate, limiting or removing the impact to your application?

Focus #2: Always Think About Scaling

Just because your application works now does not mean it will work tomorrow. Most web applications have increasing traffic patterns. A website that generates a certain amount of traffic today might generate significantly more traffic sooner than you anticipate. As you build your system, don't build it for today's traffic; build it for tomorrow's traffic.

Specifically, this might mean:

- Architect in the ability to increase the size and capacity of your databases.
- Think about what logical limits exist to your data scaling. What happens when your database tops out in its capabilities? Identify and remove these limits before your usage approaches them.
- Build your application so that you can add additional application servers easily. This often involves being observant of where and how state is maintained and of how traffic is routed.
- Redirect static traffic to offline providers. This allows your system to deal only with the dynamic traffic that it is designed to deal with. Using external content delivery networks (CDNs) not only can reduce the traffic your network has to handle but also allows the efficiencies of scale that CDNs provide to get that static content to your customers more quickly.
- Think about whether specific pieces of dynamic content can actually be generated statically. Often, content that appears dynamic is actually mostly static, and the scalability of your application can be increased by making this content static. This "dynamic that can be static" data is sometimes hidden where you don't expect it.

Is It Static, or Is It Dynamic?

Often, content that seems dynamic is actually mostly static. Think about a typical top banner on a simple website. Frequently, this content is mostly static, but occasionally there is some dynamic content included in it. For example, the top of the page might say "Log in" if you are not logged in, and "Hello, Lee" if you are logged in (assuming your name is Lee).

Does that mean the entire page must be generated dynamically? Not necessarily. With the exception of the login/greeting portion of the page, the page (or page portion) is static and can easily be provided by a CDN without any computation on your part.

When the majority of the banner is static, you can, in the user's browser, add the changeable content to the page dynamically (such as adding "Log in" or "Hello, Lee" as appropriate). By grouping this dynamic data together and processing it separately from the truly static data, you can increase the performance of your web page and decrease the amount of dynamic work your application has to perform. This increases scalability and, ultimately, availability.

Focus #3: Mitigate Risk

Keeping a system highly available requires removing risk from the system. Often the cause of a system failure could have been identified as a risk before the failure actually occurred. Identifying risk is a key method of increasing availability. All systems have risk in them. There is risk that:

- A server will crash
- A database will become corrupted
- A returned answer will be incorrect
- A network connection will fail
- A newly deployed piece of software will fail

Keeping a system available requires removing risk. But as systems become more and more complicated, this becomes less and less possible. Keeping a large system available is more about managing what your risk is, how much risk is acceptable, and what you can do to mitigate that risk.

We call this risk management. We will be talking extensively about risk management in Chapter 9. Risk management is at the heart of building highly available systems.

Part of risk management is risk mitigation. Risk mitigation is knowing what to do when a problem occurs in order to reduce the impact of the problem as much as possible. Mitigation is about making sure your application works as well and as completely as possible, even when services and resources fail. Risk mitigation requires thinking about the things that can go wrong and putting a plan together *now* so that you will be able to handle the situation when it does happen.

Risk Mitigation: The No-Search Web Store

Imagine a web store that sells T-shirts. It's your typical online store that provides the ability to browse shirts on a home page, navigate to browse different categories of shirts, and search for a specific style or type of shirt.

To implement the search capability, a store such as this typically needs to invoke a separate search engine, which may be a separate service or may even be a third-party search provider.

However, because the search capability is an independent capability, there is risk to your application that the search service will not be able to function. Your risk management plan identifies this issue and lists "Failed Search Engine" as a risk to your application.

Without a risk mitigation plan, a failed search service might simply generate an error page or perhaps generate incorrect or invalid results—in either case, it is a bad customer experience.

A risk mitigation plan for this example may say something like this:

> We know that our most popular T-shirts are our red-striped T-shirts; 60 percent of people who search our site end up looking at (and hopefully eventually buy) our famous red-striped shirts. So if our search service stops functioning, we will show an "I'm Sorry" page, followed by a list of our most popular T-shirts, including our red-striped shirts. This will encourage customers who encounter this error page to continue to browse to shirts customers have historically found as interesting.

> Additionally, we will show a "10% off next purchase" coupon, so that customers who can't find what they are looking for will be enticed to come back to our site in the future when our search service is functional again, rather than looking elsewhere.

The preceding sidebar is an example of risk mitigation; the process of identifying the risk, determining what to do, and implementing these mitigations is risk management.

This process will often uncover unknown problems in your application that you will want to fix immediately instead of waiting for them to occur. It also can create processes and procedures to handle known failure modes so that the cost of that failure is reduced in duration or severity.

Availability and risk management go hand in hand. Building a highly available system is significantly about managing risk.

Focus #4: Monitor Availability

You can't know if there is a problem in your application unless you can see a problem. Make sure your application is properly instrumented so that you can see how the application is performing from an external perspective as well as by way of internal monitoring.

Proper monitoring depends on the specifics of your application and needs, but it usually entails some of the following capabilities:

Server monitoring
> To monitor the health of your servers and make sure they keep operating efficiently.

Configuration change monitoring
> To monitor your system configuration and identify if and when changes to your infrastructure impact your application.

Application performance monitoring
> To look inside your application and services to make sure they are operating as expected.

Synthetic testing
> To examine in real time how your application is functioning from the perspective of your users, in order to catch problems customers might see before they actually see them.

Alerting
> To inform appropriate personnel when a problem occurs so that it can be quickly and efficiently resolved, minimizing the impact on your customers.

There are many good monitoring systems available, both free and paid services. I personally recommend New Relic. It provides all of the aforementioned monitoring and alerting capabilities. As a Software as a Service (SaaS) offering, it can support your monitoring needs at pretty much any scale your application may require.

After you have started monitoring your application and services, start looking for trends in your performance. When you have identified the trends, you can look for outliers and treat them as potential availability issues. You can use these outliers by having your monitoring tools send you an alert when they are identified, before your application fails. Additionally, you can track as your system grows and make sure your scalability plan will continue to work.

Establish internal, private operational goals for service-to-service communications, and monitor them continuously. This way, when you see a performance- or availability-related problem, you can quickly diagnose which service or system is responsible and address the problem. Additionally, you can see "hot spots"—areas in which your performance is not what it could be—and put development plans in place to address these issues.

Focus #5: Respond to Availability Issues in a Predictable and Defined Way

Monitoring systems are useless unless you are prepared to act on the issues that arise. This means being alerted when problems occur so that you can take action. Additionally, you should establish processes and procedures that your team can follow to help diagnose issues and easily fix common failure scenarios.

For example, if a service becomes unresponsive, you might have a set of remedies to try to make the service responsive. This might include tasks such as running a test to help diagnose where the problem is, restarting a daemon that is known to cause the service to become unresponsive, or rebooting a server if all else fails. Having standard processes in place for handling common failure scenarios will decrease the amount of time your system is unavailable. Additionally, these processes can provide useful follow-up diagnostic information to your engineering teams to help them deduce the root cause of common ailments.

When an alert is triggered for a service, the owners of that service must be the first ones alerted. They are, after all, the ones responsible for fixing any issues with their service. However, other teams who are closely connected to the troubled service and depend on it might also want to be alerted of problems when they occur. For example, if a team makes use of a particular service, they may want to know when that service fails so that they can potentially be more proactive in keeping their systems active during the dependent service outage.

These standard processes and procedures should be part of an online support manual available to all team members who handle on-call responsibility. These support artifacts should also contain contact lists for owners of related services and systems as well as contacts to call to escalate the problem if a simple solution is not possible. There are SaaS applications available that can automate the management and versioning of these support documents and make them available on demand during events.

All of these processes, procedures, and support manuals should be prepared ahead of time so that during an outage your on-call personnel know exactly what to do in various circumstances to restore operations quickly. These processes and procedures are especially useful because outages often occur during inconvenient times, such as the middle of the night or weekends—times when your on-call team might not perform at peak mental efficiency. These recommendations will assist your team in making smarter and safer moves toward restoring your system to operational status.

Being Prepared

No one can anticipate where and when availability issues will occur. But you can assume that they will occur, especially as your system scales to larger customer demands and more complex applications. Being prepared in advance to handle availability concerns is the best way to reduce the likelihood and severity of problems. The information in this chapter, including the five focuses, offers a solid strategy for keeping your applications highly available.

Two Mistakes High—Having Room to Recover from Mistakes

Consider the following anecdote I once overheard:

> We were wondering how changing a setting on our MySQL database might impact our performance, but we were worried that the change might cause our production database to fail. Because we didn't want to bring down production, we decided to make the change to our backup (replica) database instead. After all, it wasn't being used for anything at the moment.

Makes sense, right? Have you ever heard this rationale before?

Well, the problem here is that the database *was* being used for something. It was being used to provide a backup for production. Except it couldn't be used that way anymore.

You see, the backup database was essentially being used as an experimental playground for trying different types of settings. The net result was that the backup database began to drift away from the primary production database as settings began to change over time.

Then, one day, the inevitable happened.

The production database failed.

The backup database initially did what it was supposed to do. It took over the job of the primary database. Except it really couldn't. The settings on the backup database had wandered so far away from those required by the primary database that it could no longer reliably handle the same traffic load that the primary database handled.

The backup database slowly failed, and the site went down.

This is a true story. It's a story about best intentions. You have a backup, replicated database on standby. It's ready to take over as needed when the primary database fails. But because the backup database isn't treated with the same respect as the primary database, it loses the ability to perform its main purpose, that of being the backup database.

Two wrongs don't make a right, two mistakes don't negate each other, and two problems don't self-correct. A primary database failure along with a poorly managed backup server does not create a good day.

How can we avoid these types of availability concerns? There is an answer that comes from the world of radio control airplanes.

Two Mistakes High

If you've ever flown radio control (R/C) airplanes before, you might have heard the expression "keep your plane two mistakes high." When you learn to fly R/C planes, and especially when you begin learning how to do acrobatics, you learn this quickly. You see, mistakes equate to altitude. If you make a mistake, you lose altitude. You lose too much altitude, and you crash. Keeping your plane "two mistakes high" means keeping it high enough that you have enough altitude to recover from two independent mistakes.

Think about it: during your recovery process, you are typically stressed and perhaps in an awkward situation doing potentially abnormal things—just the type of situation that can cause you to make another mistake. If you aren't high enough, you can crash.

Put another way, if you normally fly two mistakes high, you can always have a backup plan for recovering from a mistake, even if you are currently recovering from a different mistake.

This same philosophy is important to understand when building highly available, high-scale applications.

How do we "keep two mistakes high" in an application? For starters, when we identify the failure scenarios that we anticipate our application facing, we walk through the ramifications of those scenarios and our recovery plan for them. We make sure the recovery plan itself does not have mistakes or other shortcomings built into it—in short, we check that the recovery plan is able to work. If we find that it doesn't work, then it's not a recovery plan.

This is just one potential scenario in which "two mistakes" applies. There are many more. Let's take a look at some example scenarios to see how this philosophy plays out in our applications.

Scenario #1: Losing a Node

Let's look at an example scenario involving traffic to a web service.

Suppose that you're building a service that is designed to handle 1,000 requests per second (req/sec). Further, let's assume that a single node in your service can handle 300 req/sec.

Question: How many nodes do you need to handle your traffic demands?

Some basic math should come up with a good answer:

number_of_nodes_needed = ⌈number_of_requests / requests_per_node⌉

where:

number_of_nodes_needed
   The number of nodes needed to handle the specified number of requests.

number_of_requests
   The design limit for the number of requests the service is expected to happen.

requests_per_node
   The expected average number of requests each node in the service can handle.

Putting in our numbers:

number_of_nodes_needed = ⌈1,000 req/sec / 300 req/sec⌉ = ⌈3.3⌉ = 4 nodes

number_of_nodes_needed = 4 nodes

You need four nodes in your service to handle the 1,000 req/sec expected service load. Switching this around, using four nodes, each node will handle:

requests_per_node = number_of_requests / number_of_nodes

requests_per_node = 1,000 req/sec / 4 nodes = 250 req/sec/node

Each node will handle 250 req/sec, which is well below your 300 req/sec node limit (see Figure 2-1).

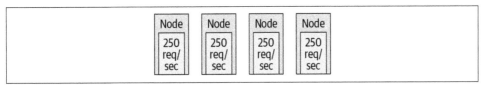

Figure 2-1. Four nodes, 250 req/sec each

You have four nodes in your system. You can handle the expected traffic, and because you have four nodes, you can handle the loss of a node. You have built in the ability to handle a node failure. Right? Right???

Well, no, not really. If you lose a node at peak traffic, your service will begin to fail. Why? Because if you lose a node, the rest of your traffic must be spread among the remaining three nodes. So:

requests_per_node = number_of_requests / number_of_nodes

requests_per_node = 1,000 req/sec / 3 nodes = 333 req/sec/node

That's 333 req/sec per node, which is well above your 300 req/sec node limit (see Figure 2-2).

Because each node can handle only 300 req/sec, you have overloaded your servers. Either you will give poor performance to all your customers, or you will drop some requests, or you will begin to fail in other ways. In any case, you will begin to lose availability.

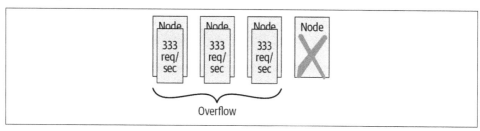

Figure 2-2. Four nodes; one failure causes overflow

As you can see from Figure 2-2, if you lose a node in your system, you cannot continue to operate at full capacity. So even though you think you can recover from a node failure, you really can't. You are vulnerable.

To handle a node failure, you need more than four nodes. If you want to be able to handle a single node failure, you need five nodes. That way, if one of the five nodes fails, you still have four remaining nodes to handle the load:

requests_per_node = number_of_requests / number_of_nodes

requests_per_node = 1,000 req/sec / 4 nodes = 250 req/sec/node

This is illustrated in Figure 2-3. Because 250 req/sec is below the node limit of 300 req/sec, there is enough capacity to continue handling all of your traffic, even with a single node failure.

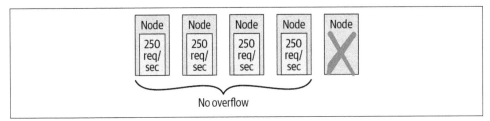

Figure 2-3. Five nodes; one failure can still be handled

Scenario #2: Problems During Upgrades

Another example of two mistakes high in our applications happens during upgrades. Upgrades and other routine maintenance can cause availability problems beyond just the obvious.

Suppose that you have a service whose average traffic is 1,000 req/sec. Further, let's assume that a single node in your service can handle 300 req/sec. As discussed in the preceding example, four nodes is the required minimum to run your service. To handle the expected traffic and to be able to handle a single node failure, you give your service five nodes with which to handle the load.

Now suppose that you want to do a software upgrade to the service running on the nodes. To keep your service operating at full capacity during the upgrade, you decide to do a rolling deploy.

Put simply, a rolling deploy means that you upgrade one node at a time (temporarily taking it offline to perform the upgrade). After the first node has been upgraded successfully and is handling traffic again, you move on to upgrade the second node (temporarily taking it offline). You continue until all five nodes are upgraded.

Because only one node is offline to be upgraded at any point in time, there are always at least four nodes handling traffic. Because four nodes is enough to handle all of your traffic, your service stays up and operational during the upgrade.

This is a great plan. You've built a system that not only can handle a single node failure but also can be upgraded by rolling deploys without having any downtime.

But what happens if a single node failure occurs during an upgrade? In that case, you have one node unavailable for the upgrade and one failed node. That leaves only three nodes to handle all your traffic, which is not enough. You are experiencing a service degradation or outage.

But what's the likelihood of a node failure occurring during an upgrade?

How many times have you had an upgrade fail? In fact, an argument can be made that you are more prone to node failures around the time of an upgrade than at any other point in time. The upgrade and the node failure do not have to be independent of each other.

 The lesson is this: even if you think you have redundancy to handle different failure modes, if it is likely that two or more problems can occur at the same time (because the problems are correlated), you essentially do not have redundancy at all. You are prone to an availability issue.

So to handle the 1,000 req/sec expected traffic using nodes that can handle 300 req/sec each, we will need at least:

Four nodes
Which can handle the traffic but will not handle a node failure.

Five nodes
Which handle a single node failure, or make it possible for a node to be unavailable for maintenance or upgrade.

Six nodes
Which can handle a multinode failure, or make it possible for you to survive a single node failure while another node is down for maintenance or upgrade.

Scenario #3: Data Center Resiliency

Let's scale the problem up a bit and take a look at data center redundancy and resilience.

Suppose that your service is now handling 10,000 req/sec. With single nodes handling 300 req/sec, that means you need 34 nodes, without considering redundancy for failures and upgrades.

Let's add a bunch of resiliency and use a total of 40 nodes (each handling 250 req/sec), which allows for plenty of extra capacity. We could lose up to six nodes and still handle our full capacity.

Let's do an even better job: let's split those 40 nodes evenly across four data centers so that we have even more redundancy.

So now we are resilient to data center outages as well as node failures. This is illustrated in Figure 2-4.

We are properly resilient, right?

Well, no, we are not. Obviously we can handle individual node outages, because we have given ourselves 6 (40 − 34) extra nodes. But what if a data center goes offline?

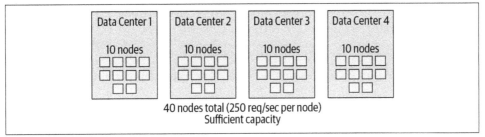

Figure 2-4. Four data centers, 40 nodes, sufficient capacity to handle load

If a single data center fails, we lose one quarter of our servers. In this example, we would go from 40 nodes to 30 nodes. The nodes no longer must handle traffic of 250 req/sec per node; rather, each node now needs to handle 333 req/sec. This is illustrated in Figure 2-5. Because this is more than the capacity of your fictitious nodes, you have an availability issue.

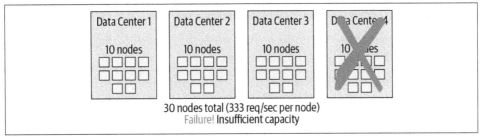

Figure 2-5. Four data centers, one failed, 30 nodes, insufficient capacity to handle load

Although we are using multiple data centers, a failure of just one of those data centers would leave us in a situation where we wouldn't be able to handle increased traffic. We think we are resilient to a data center loss, but we are not.

Then how many servers do you need?

How many servers do we need to have the ability to lose a data center? Let's find out.

Using the same assumptions, we know that we need a minimum of 34 working servers to handle all of our traffic. If we are using four data centers, how many servers do we need to have true data center redundancy?

Well, we need to make sure we always have 34 working servers, even if one of the four data centers goes down. This means that we need to have 34 servers spread across three data centers:

nodes_per_data_center = $\lceil$min_number_of_servers / (number_of_data_centers − 1)$\rceil$

nodes_per_data_center = $\lceil$34 / (4 − 1)$\rceil$

nodes_per_data_center = $\lceil$11.333$\rceil$ = 12 servers/data_center

Because we need 12 servers per data center, and because any one of the four data centers could go offline, we need 12 in each data center:

total_nodes = nodes_per_data_center × 4 = 48 nodes

We need 48 nodes to guarantee that we have 34 working servers in the case of a data center outage.

How does changing the number of data centers change our calculation? What if we have two data centers? As before:

nodes_per_data_center = $\lceil$min_number_of_servers / (number_of_data_centers − 1)$\rceil$

nodes_per_data_center = $\lceil$34 / (2 − 1)$\rceil$

nodes_per_data_center = 34

total_nodes = nodes_per_data_center × 2 = 68 nodes

If we have two data centers, we need 68 nodes to maintain data center redundancy. If we have four data centers, we need 48 nodes to maintain data center redundancy. If we have six data centers, we need 42 nodes to maintain data center redundancy.

Notice the number of needed nodes goes down as the number of data centers goes up. This demonstrates a seemingly odd conclusion:

> To ensure the ability to recover from a data center outage, the more data centers you have, the fewer nodes you need overall spread across those data centers.

This seems backwards. So much for natural intuition. There is a lesson we can take from this. Although the details of this demonstration might not directly apply to a real-world situation, the point still applies. *Be careful when you devise your resiliency plans. Your intuition might not match reality, and if your intuition is wrong, you are prone to an availability issue.* If you used intuition alone in the preceding example, either you would not have enough nodes to handle a data center failure in any circumstance, or you'd end up with more nodes than is required to get the level of resiliency desired.

Scenario #4: Hidden Shared Failure Types

Sometimes, multiple problem scenarios that seem to be independent and not likely to occur together are, in fact, dependent scenarios. This means that they could and in some situations reasonably should be expected to fail together.

Suppose that your service runs on four nodes. You are trying to think ahead, so you use a total of six nodes—enough to handle both a single node failure and an upgrade in progress.

You're all set. Your system is safe.

Then it happens: in your data center, a power supply in a rack goes bad, and the rack goes dark.

It's usually about this time that you realize that all six of your servers are in the same rack. How do you discover this? Because all six servers go down, and your service is completely down.

There goes redundancy...

Even when you think you are safe, you might not be. We know that not all problems are independent of one another. But this is a case where a potentially unseen, or at least unnoticed, commonality exists among all your servers: they all share the same rack and the same power supply for that rack.

Make sure to check for the hidden shared failure modes that can cause your carefully laid plans to be wrong, thus making you prone to an availability issue.

Scenario #5: Failure Loops

A failure loop is when a specific problem causes your system to fail in a way that makes it difficult or impossible for you to fix the problem without causing a worse problem to occur.

The best way to explain this is with a non-server-based example. Suppose you live in a great apartment that even provides an enclosed garage for you to store things in! Wow, you are set. But the power in the place goes out a lot, so you decide to buy a generator that you can use when the power does go out. You take the generator, and the gas it uses, and you store it in the garage. Life is good.

Then, when the power goes out, you go to get your generator. That's when you realize for the first time that the only way to access your garage is through the electric-powered garage door—the one that doesn't work because the power is out.

Oops.

Just because you have a backup plan does not mean you can implement the backup plan when needed.

The same issues can apply to our service world. Can a service failure make it difficult to repair that same service because it caused some other seemingly unrelated issue to occur? For example, if your service fails, how easy is it to deploy an updated version of your service? What happens if your service-deployment service fails? What if the service you use to monitor the performance of other services fails?

Make sure the plans you have for recovering from a problem can be implemented even when the problem is occurring. Dependent relationships between the problem and the solution to the problem can make you prone to an availability issue.

Managing Your Applications

"Fly two mistakes high" in our context means *don't just look for the surface failure modes.* Look the next level down. Make sure that you do not have dependent failure modes and that the recovery mechanisms you have put in place will, in fact, recover your system while a failure is going on.

Additionally, don't ignore problems. They don't go away, and they can interfere with your predicted availability plans. Just because the database that fails is only the backup database doesn't mean it isn't mission critical to fix. Treat your backup and redundant systems just as preciously as you treat your primary systems. After all, they are just as important.

As a friend of mine is often heard to say, "If it touches production, it is production." Don't take anything in production for granted.

This stuff is difficult. It isn't at all obvious to know when you have these types of layered or dependent failures. Take the time to look at your situations and resolve them.

The Space Shuttle

Let's end this chapter with a great example of an independent, redundant, multilevel error-recoverable system. In fact, it was one of the very first large-scale software applications that utilized extreme principles of redundancy and failure management. It had to—the astronauts' lives depended on it.

I'm referring to the United States Space Shuttle program.

The Space Shuttle program had some significant and serious mechanical problems, which we won't fully address here. But the software system built into the Space Shuttle utilized state-of-the art techniques for redundancy and independent error recovery.

The primary computer system of the Space Shuttle consisted of five computers. Four of them were identical computers with identical software running on them, but the fifth was different. We'll discuss that later.

The four main computers all ran the exact same program during critical parts of the mission (such as launch and landing). These four computers were all given the same data and had the same software, and so they were expected to generate the same results. All four performed the same calculations, and they constantly compared the results. If, at any point in time, one or more of the computers generated a different result, the four computers voted on which result was correct. The winning result was used, and the computer(s) that generated the losing result was turned off for the duration of the flight. The shuttle could successfully fly with only three computers turned on, and it could safely land with only two operational computers.

Talk about the ultimate in democratic systems. The winners rule, and the losers are terminated.

But what would happen if the four computers couldn't agree? This could happen if there were multiple failures and multiple computers had been shut down. Or it could happen if a serious software glitch in the main software affected all four computers at the same time (the four computers were running the exact same software, after all).

This is where the fifth computer came into play. It normally sat idle, but if needed, it could perform the exact same calculations as the other four. The key was the software it ran. The software for the fifth system was a much simpler version of the software that was built by a completely independent group of programmers. In theory, it could not have the same software errors as the main software.

So if the main software and the four main computers could not agree on a result, the final result was left to the fifth, completely independent computer.

This is a highly redundant, high-availability system with a high level of separation between potential problems.

During its 30 years of operation, the Space Shuttle program never experienced a serious life-threatening problem during any of its missions that was a result of the failure of the software or the computers the software ran on—even though the software was, at the time, the most complex software system ever built for a space program.

PART II

Tenet 2. Modern Application Architecture: Using Services

Modern software requires the use of modern application architectures. Modern application architectures require moving away from monolithic applications and embracing service-based architectures.

Monolith applications are extremely hard to scale, both from a traffic scaling standpoint and from the standpoint of your ability to scale the size of your organization to work on the application. The larger the monolith, the slower it is to make changes to the application, the fewer the people who can work on it and manage it effectively, and the greater the likelihood that traffic variations and growth will negatively impact availability.

Service-oriented architectures solve these problems by providing greater flexibility in scaling based on traffic needs, as well as providing a scalable framework to allow larger development organizations to work on the application, thus allowing the applications themselves to get larger and more complex.

CHAPTER 3

Using Services

Modern software requires the use of modern application architectures, but what is involved in modern software architectures? One of the keys to architecting highly scaled and highly available applications is to utilize service- or microservice-based architectures. Legacy monolithic application development processes do not provide you the capabilities you need to keep your application running at scale and maintain availability.

Historically, most applications appear as single, large, distinct monoliths. The single monolith encompasses all business activities for a single application. To implement an improved piece of business functionality, an individual developer must make changes within the single application, and all developers making changes must make them within the same single application. Developers can easily step on one another's toes and make conflicting changes that result in problems and outages.

In a service-oriented architecture, individual services are created that encompass a specific subset of business logic. These individual services are interconnected to provide the entire set of business logic for the application.

Let's compare monolith and service-oriented architectures and see why service-oriented architectures provide better organizational scalability and application scalability.

The Monolith Application Versus the Service-Based Application

A traditional large monolithic application contains all logic and functionality within a single component, with individual code segments intertwined and dependent on each other. It's a single compiled piece of source that creates a single executable containing most or all aspects of the application. Figure 3-1 shows an application that represents a monolith.

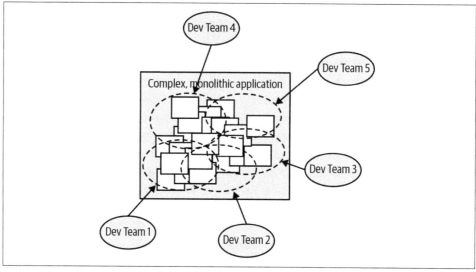

Figure 3-1. A large, complex monolithic application

This is how most applications begin to look if they are constructed and grow as monolithic applications. In Figure 3-1, you see that there are five independent development teams working on overlapping areas of the application. It is impossible to know who is working on what piece of the application at any point in time, and code-change collisions and problems are easy to imagine. Code quality and hence application quality and availability suffer. Additionally, it becomes more and more difficult for individual development teams to make changes without having to deal with the effect of other teams, incompatible changes, and a molasses effect on the organization as a whole.

Figure 3-2 presents the same application constructed as a series of services. Each service has a clear owner. Each team has a clear, nonoverlapping set of responsibilities.

Service-oriented architectures provide the ability to split an application into distinct domains that are each managed by individual groups within your organization. They enable the separation of responsibilities that are critical for building highly scaled applications, allowing work to be done independently on individual services without affecting the work of other groups working on the same overall application.

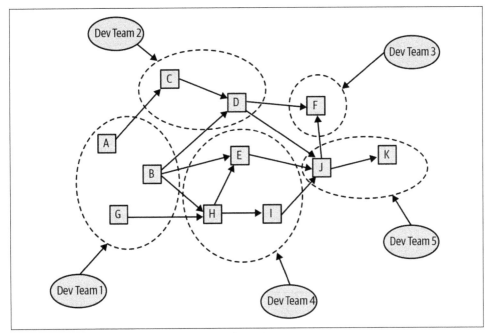

Figure 3-2. A large, complex service-based application

When building highly scaled applications, service-based application architectures provide the following benefits:

Scaling decisions
Service-based architectures make it possible for scaling decisions to be made at a more granular level, which fosters more efficient system optimization and organization.

Team assignment and focus
Service-based architectures let you assign capabilities to individual teams in such a way that teams can focus on the specific scaling and availability requirements of their system "in the small" and feel confident that their decisions will have the appropriate impact at the larger scale.

Complexity localization
Using service-based architectures, you can think about services as black boxes, making it so that only the owners of a particular service need to understand the complexity within that service. Other developers need to know only the capabilities that service provides, without knowing anything about how it works internally. This compartmenting of knowledge and complexity facilitates the creation of larger applications since individual teams need to understand only their

individual subsets of the application. This lets you manage these larger applications more effectively.

Testing

Service-based architectures are easier to test than monolithic applications, which increases your reliability.

Service-oriented architectures can, however, increase the complexity of your system as a whole if the service boundaries are not designed properly. This complexity can lead to lower scalability and decreased system availability. So picking the appropriate service and service boundaries is critical.

The Ownership Benefit

Let's take a look at a pair of services.

In Figure 3-3, we see two services owned by two distinct teams. The Left Service is consuming the capabilities exposed by the Right Service.

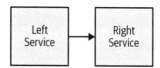

Figure 3-3. A pair of services

Let's look at this diagram from the perspective of the Left Service owner. Obviously that team needs to know the entire structure, complexity, connectedness, interactions, code, and so on for its service. But what does it need to know about the Right Service? As a start, the team needs to know the following:

- The capabilities provided by the service
- How to call those capabilities (the API syntax)
- The meanings and results of calling those capabilities (the API semantics)

That's the basic information that the Left Service team needs to know. What doesn't it need to know about the Right Service? Lots of things—for example:

- The Left Service team does not need to know whether the Right Service is a single service or a construction of many subservices.
- It does not need to know what services the Right Service depends on to perform its responsibilities.
- It does not need to know what language(s) the Right Service is written in.

- It does not need to know what hardware or system infrastructure is needed to operate the Right Service.

- It does not even need to know who is operating the Right Service (however, it does need to know how to contact the owner of the Right Service in case there are issues with it).

The Right Service can be as complex or as simple as needed, as shown in Figure 3-4. But to the owners of the Left Service, the Right Service can be thought of as nothing more than a black box, as shown in Figure 3-5. As long as the Left Service owners know what the interface to the box is (the API), they can use the capabilities the black box provides.

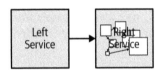

Figure 3-4. What's inside the Right Service

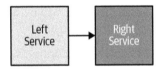

Figure 3-5. Right Service complexity hidden from dependencies

To manage this, the Left Service must be able to depend on a contract that the Right Service provides. This contract describes everything the Left Service needs to use the Right Service.

The contract contains two parts:

The capabilities of the service (the API)
What the service does
How to call it and what each call means

The responsiveness of the service
How often can the API be used?
When can it be used?
How fast will the API respond?
Is the API dependable?

All of this information describes the contract that the owners of the Right Service provide to the Left Service describing how the Right Service operates. As long as the

Right Service behaves according to this contract, the Left Service doesn't have to know or care anything about how the Right Service performs those commitments.

The responsiveness part of the contract is called a service-level agreement, or SLA. It is a critical component in allowing the Left Service to depend on the Right Service without knowing anything about how the Right Service works. We discuss SLAs in great detail in Chapter 8.

By having a clear ownership for each service, teams can focus on only those portions of the system for which they are responsible, along with the API contracts provided by the owners of the services they depend on. This separation of responsibility makes it easier to scale your organization to contain many more teams; because the coupling between the teams is substantially looser, it doesn't matter as much how far away (organizationally or physically) one team is from another. As long as the contracts are maintained, you can scale your organization as needed to build larger and more complicated applications.

The Scaling Benefit

Different parts of your application have different scaling needs. The component that generates the home page of your application will be used much more often than the component that generates the user settings page.

By using services with clear APIs and API contracts between them, you can determine and implement the scaling needs required for each service independently. This means that if your home page is the most frequently called page, you can provide more hardware to run that service than you provide for the service that manages your user settings page.

Managing the scaling needs of each service independently enables you to do the following:

- Provide more accurate scaling by having the team that owns the specific capability involved closely in the scaling decision.
- Save system resources by not scaling one component simply because another component requires it.
- Provide ownership of scaling decisions to the team that knows the most about the needs of the service (the service owner).

Service-based architectures make scaling your organization and your application easier, allowing you to scale to a greater level. In the next chapter, we examine services in greater detail.

Splitting into Services

A service provides some capabilities that are needed by the rest of the application. Examples include billing services (which offer the component that bills customers), account creation services (which manage the component that creates accounts), and notification services (which include functionality for notifying users of events and conditions).

A service is a standalone component. The word *standalone* is critical. A service meets the following criteria:

Maintains its own code base
A service has its own code base that is distinct from the rest of your code base.

Manages its own data
A service that requires maintaining state has its own data that is stored in its own data store. The only access to this separated data is via the service's defined API. No other service may directly touch another service's data or state information.

Provides capabilities to others
A service has a well-defined set of capabilities, and it provides these capabilities to other services in your application. In other words, it provides an API.

Consumes capabilities from others
A service uses a well-defined set of capabilities provided by others and uses them in a standard, supported manner. In other words, it uses other services' APIs.

Single owner
A service is owned and maintained by a single development team within your organization. A single team may own and maintain more than one service, but a single service can have only one team that owns and maintains it.

What Should Be a Service?

How do you decide when a piece of an application or system should be separated out into its own service?

This is a good question, and it's one that does not have a single correct answer. Some companies that "service-ize" split their application into many very tiny microservices (hundreds or thousands of them). Others split their application into only a handful of larger services. There is no right answer to this problem. However, the industry is trending toward smaller microservices, and more of them. Technologies such as Docker and Kubernetes have made this increased number of microservices a more viable system topology by providing an infrastructure for managing a large number of small services.

We use the terms *services* and *microservices* interchangeably in this book.

Dividing into Services

So how do you decide where service boundaries should be? Company organization, culture, and the type of application can play a major role in determining service boundaries.

Following is a set of guidelines that you can use to determine where service boundaries can be. These are guidelines, not rules, and they are likely to change over time as our industry progresses. They are useful to help individuals begin thinking about services and about what should be a service.

Here at a high level are the guidelines (in order of priority):

Specific business requirements
> Are there any specific business requirements (such as accounting, security, or regulatory) that drive where a service boundary should be?

Distinct and separable team ownership
> Is the team that owns the functionality distinct and separable (such as in another city, on another floor, or even just under a different manager), which will help specify where a boundary should be?

Naturally separable data
> Is the data the service manages naturally separable from other data used in the system? Does putting data in a separate data store overly burden the system?

Shared capabilities/data
> Does it provide some shared capabilities used by lots of other services, and does that shared capability require shared data?

Let's now look at each of these individually and figure out what they mean.

Guideline #1: Specific Business Requirements

In some cases, there will be specific business requirements that dictate where a service boundary should be. These might be regulatory, legal, or security requirements, or some critical business need.

Imagine your system accepts online credit card payments from your customers. How should you collect, process, and store these credit cards and the payments they represent? A good business strategy would be to put the credit card processing in a different service, separate from the rest of the system.

Putting critical business logic into its own service can be a valuable separation to make. For credit card processing, for example, this may be true for several reasons:

Legal/regulatory requirements
There are legal and regulatory requirements around how you store credit cards that require you to treat them in different ways from other business logic and other business data. Separating credit card processing into a distinct service makes it easier to treat this data differently from the rest of your business data.

Security
You might need additional firewalls around these servers for security reasons.

Validation
You might need to perform additional production testing to verify security of these capabilities in ways significantly stronger than other parts of your system.

Restricting access
You will typically want to restrict access to these servers so that only necessary personnel have access to highly sensitive payment information such as credit cards. You typically do not want or need to provide access to these systems to your entire engineering organization.

Understanding the needs of critical business logic is an important consideration for deciding where service boundaries should be.

Guideline #2: Distinct and Separable Team Ownership

Applications are becoming more and more complicated, and typically larger groups of developers are working on them, often with more specialized responsibilities. Coordination among teams becomes substantially harder as the number of developers, the number of teams, and the number of development locations grow.

Services are a way to give ownership of smaller, distinct, separable modules to different teams.

A single service should be owned and operated by a single team that is typically no larger than three to eight developers. That team should be responsible for all aspects of that service.

By doing this, you loosen up the interteam dependencies and make it much easier for individual teams to operate and innovate independently from one another.

As previously stated, a single service should be owned and operated by a single team. The key is to make sure that all aspects of a single service are under the influence of a single team. This means that team is responsible for all development, testing, deployment, performance, and availability aspects of that service.

A single team can successfully manage more than one service, depending on the complexity and activity involved in those services. Additionally, if several services are very similar in nature, it might be easier for a single team to manage all of them.

Separate team for security reasons

Sometimes you want to restrict the number and scope of individuals who have access to the code and data stored within a given service. This is especially true for services that have regulatory or legal constraints, such as the credit card payment processing discussed before. Limiting access to a service with sensitive data can decrease your exposure to issues involved in the compromising of that data. In cases like this, you might physically limit access to the code, the data, and the systems hosting the service to only the key personnel required to support that service.

Additionally, splitting related sensitive data into two or more services, each owned by distinct teams, can reduce the chances of that data being compromised by making it less likely that multiple services with distinct owners will all have data compromised.

Splitting Data for Security Reasons

When you are processing credit card payments, the credit card numbers themselves can be stored in one service. The secondary information necessary to use those credit cards (such as billing address and CCV code) could be stored in a second service. By splitting this information across two services, each owned and operated by individual teams, you limit the chance that any one employee can inadvertently or intentionally expose enough data for a rogue agent to use one of your customers' credit cards inappropriately.

You might even choose to not store the credit card numbers in your services at all and instead store them in a third-party credit card processing company's services. This ensures that, even if one of your services is compromised, the credit cards themselves will not be.

Guideline #3: Naturally Separable Data

One of the requirements for a service is that its managed state and data need to be separate from other data. For a variety of reasons, it is problematic to have multiple independent code bases operating on the same set of data. Separating the code and the ownership is effective only if you also separate the data.

Figure 3-6 shows a service (Service A) that is trying to access data stored in another service (Service B). It illustrates the correct way for Service A to access data stored in Service B, which is for Service A to make an API call to Service B and then let Service B access the data in its database itself.

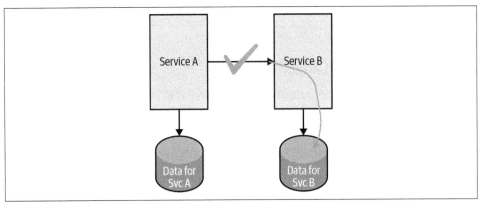

Figure 3-6. Correct way to share data

If Service A instead tries to access the data for Service B directly without going through Service B's API, as shown in Figure 3-7, all sorts of problems can occur. This sort of data integration would require tighter coordination between Service A and Service B than is desired, and it can cause problems when data maintenance and schema migration activities need to occur. In general, the accessing of Service B's data directly by Service A without involving Service B's business logic in that process can cause serious data versioning and data corruption issues. It should be strictly avoided.

As you can see, determining data division lines is an important characteristic in determining service division lines. Does it make sense for a given service to be the "owner" of its data and provide access to that data only via external service interfaces? If the answer is "yes," this is a good candidate for a service boundary. If the answer is "no," it is not a good service boundary.

A service that needs to operate on data owned by another service must do so via published interfaces (APIs) provided by the service that owns that data.

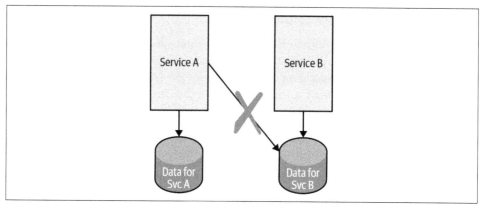

Figure 3-7. Incorrect way to share data

Guideline #4: Shared Capabilities/Data

Sometimes a service can be created simply because it is responsible for a set of capabilities and its data. These capabilities and data might need to be shared by a variety of other services.

A prime example of this principle is a user identity service, which simply provides information about specific users of the system. This is illustrated in Figure 3-8.

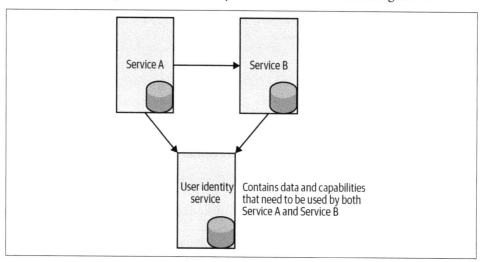

Figure 3-8. Using services to share common data with other services

There might be no complex business logic involved with this data service, but it's ultimately responsible for all the general information associated with individual users. This information often is used by a large number of other services.

Having a centralized service that provides and manages this single piece of information is highly useful.

Mixed Reasons

The preceding guidelines outline some basic criteria for determining where service boundaries should be. Often, though, it is a combination of reasons that can ultimately make the decision for you.

For example, having a single user identity service makes sense from a data ownership and shared capabilities perspective, but it might not make sense from a team ownership standpoint. Data for which it might make sense to store it in a database associated with user identity might be better stored in a separate service or services.

As a specific example of such data, a user may have search preferences that are typically part of a user profile but are not typically used by anything outside of the search infrastructure. As such, it might make sense to store this data in a search identity service that is distinct from a user identity service. This might be for data complexity reasons or even for performance reasons.

Ultimately, you must use your judgment while also taking the preceding criteria into account. And of course, you must also consider the business logic and requirements dictated by your company and your specific business needs.

Going Too Far

While splitting applications into services has many benefits, often you can go too far. Creating service boundaries using the previously discussed criteria can be taken to the extreme, and too many services can be created.

For example, rather than providing a simple user identity service, you might decide to take that simple service and further divide it into several smaller services, such as the following:

- User human-readable name service
- User physical address management service
- User email address management service
- User hometown management service

Doing this is most likely splitting things up too much.

There are several problems with splitting services into too fine a number of pieces, including overall application performance. But at the most fundamental level, every time you split a piece of functionality into multiple services, you do the following:

- Decrease the complexity of the individual services (usually)
- Increase the complexity of your application as a whole

The smaller service size typically makes individual services less complicated. However, the more services you have, the larger the number of independent services that need to be coordinated, and the more complex your overall application architecture becomes.

Having a system with an excessively large number of services tends to create the following problems in your application:

Big picture
It becomes more difficult to keep the entire application architecture in mind, because the application is becoming more complicated.

More failure opportunities
More independent components need to work together, creating more opportunity for interservice failures to occur.

Harder to change services
Each individual service tends to have more consumers of that service (other services that depend on it). Having more service consumers increases the likelihood of changes to your service negatively affecting one of your consumers.

More dependencies
Each individual service tends to have more dependencies on other services. More dependencies means more places for problems to occur.

Many of these problems can be mitigated by defining solid interface boundaries between services, but this is not a complete solution. Instead, it's important to find the right balance between the number of services and the size of those services.

Finding the Right Balance

Ultimately, deciding on the proper number of services and the proper size of each service is a complicated problem to solve. It requires careful consideration of the balance between the advantages of creating more services and the disadvantages of creating a more complex system as a whole.

Building too few services will create problems similar to the monolith application, where too many developers will be working on a single service and the individual services themselves become overly complicated.

Building too many services will cause individual services to become trivially simple, while the overall application becomes overly complicated by complex interactions between the services. I've actually heard of an example application utilizing microservices that defined a "Yes" service and a "No" service that simply returned those boolean results—this is extreme taken to extreme. It would be great to define exactly what the right size is for a service, but it depends on your application and your company culture. The best advice is to keep this complexity trade-off in mind as you define your services and your architecture.

Finding the appropriate balance for your specific application, organization, and company culture is important in making the most use of a service-based environment.

Determining the appropriate balance in service size is important to creating an application architecture that is optimized for operation and management and to keeping your application highly available and scalable.

CHAPTER 4

Services and Data

As you build and migrate your application to a service-based architecture, it is critically important to be mindful of where you store data and state within your application.

Stateless Services—Services Without Data

Stateless services are services that manage no data and no state of their own. The entire state and all data that the service requires to perform its actions is passed in (or referenced) in the request sent to the service.

Stateless services offer a huge advantage for scaling. Because they are stateless, it is usually an easy matter to add additional server capacity to a service in order to scale it to a larger capacity, both vertically and horizontally. You get maximum flexibility in how and when you can scale your service if your service does not maintain state.

Additionally, certain caching techniques on the frontend of the service become possible if the cache does not need to concern itself with service state. This caching lets you handle higher scaling requirements with fewer resources.

Not all services can be made stateless, obviously, but for those services that can be stateless, it is a huge advantage for scalability.

Stateful Services—Services with Data

When you do need to store data, given what we just discussed in the preceding section, it might seem obvious to store data in as few services and systems as possible. It might make sense to keep all of your data close to one another to reduce the footprint of the services that need to know and manage your data.

Nothing could be further from the truth.

Instead, localize your data as much as possible. Have services and data stores manage only the data they need to perform their jobs. Other data should be stored in different servers and data stores, closer to the services that require that data.

Localizing data this way provides a few benefits:

Reduced size of individual datasets

Because your data is split across datasets, each dataset is smaller in size. Smaller dataset size means reduced interaction with the data, making scalability of the database easier. This is called functional partitioning. You are splitting your data based on functional lines rather than on the size of the dataset.

Localized access

Frequently when you access data in a database or data store, you are accessing all the data within a given record or set of records. Often, much of that data is not needed for a given interaction. By using multiple reduced dataset sizes, you reduce the amount of unneeded data from your queries.

Optimized access methods

By splitting your data into different datasets, you can optimize the type of data store appropriate for each dataset. Does a particular dataset need a relational data store? Or is a simple key/value data store acceptable?

Keeping your data associated with the services that consume the data will create a more scalable solution, and easier-to-manage architecture and will allow your data requirements to more easily expand as your application expands.

Data Partitioning

Data partitioning can mean many things. In this context, it means partitioning data of a given type into segments based on some key or identifier within the data. It is often done to make use of multiple databases to store larger datasets or datasets accessed at a higher frequency than a single database can handle.

There are other types of data partitioning (such as the aforementioned functional partitioning); however, in this section, we are going to focus on this key-based partitioning scheme.

A simple example of data partitioning is to partition all data for an application by account, so that all data for accounts whose name begins with A–D is in one database, all data for accounts whose name begins with E–K is in another database, and so on (see Figure 4-1).[1] This is a very simplistic example, but data partitioning is a common tool used by application developers to dramatically scale the number of users who can access the application at any one time, as well as to scale the size of the dataset itself.

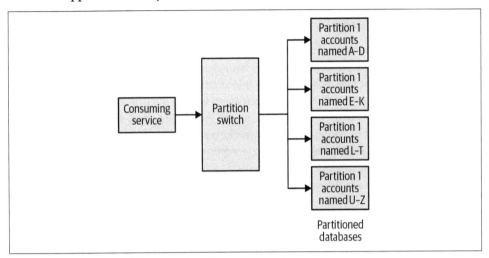

Figure 4-1. Example of data partitioning by account name

In general, you should avoid data partitioning whenever possible. Why? Well, whenever you partition data this way, you run into several potential issues:

Application complexity
  You increase the complexity of your application because you now have to determine where your data is stored before you can actually retrieve it.

Cross-partition queries
  You remove the ability to easily query data across multiple partitions. This is specifically useful in doing business analysis queries.

Skewed partition usage
  Choosing your partitioning key carefully is critical. If you choose the wrong key, you can skew the usage of your database partitions, making some partitions run hotter and others colder, thus reducing the effectiveness of the partitioning while complicating your database management and maintenance. This is illustrated in Figure 4-2.

---

1 A more likely account-based partitioning mechanism would be to partition by an account identifier rather than by account name. However, using account name makes this example easier to follow.

Repartitioning

Repartitioning is occasionally necessary to balance traffic across partitions effectively. Depending on the key chosen and the type and size of the dataset, this can prove to be an extremely difficult task, an extremely dangerous task (data migration), and in some cases, a nearly impossible task.

In general, account name or account ID is almost always a bad partition key (yet it is one of the most common keys chosen). This is because a single account can change in size during the life of that account. Take a look at Figure 4-2. An account might begin small and thus may easily fit on a partition with a significant number of small accounts. However, if it grows over time, it can soon cause that single partition to not be able to handle all of the load appropriately, and you'll need to repartition in order to better balance account usage. If a single account grows too large, it can actually be bigger than what can fit on a single partition, which will make your entire partitioning scheme fail, because no rebalancing will solve that problem.

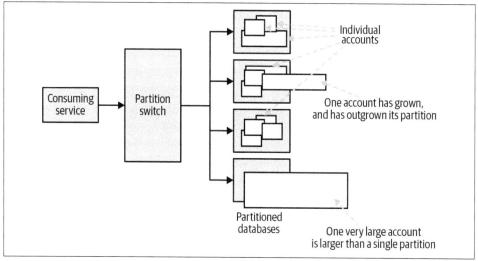

Figure 4-2. Example of accounts overrunning data partitions

A better partition key would be one that would result in consistently sized partitions as much as possible. Growth of partitions should be as independent and consistent as possible, as shown in Figure 4-3. If repartitioning is needed, it should be because all partitions have grown consistently and are too big to be handled by the database.

One potentially useful partitioning scheme is to use a key that generates a significant number of small elements. Next, map these small partitions onto larger partitioned databases. Then, if repartitioning is needed, you can simply update the mapping and move individual small elements to new partitions, removing the need for a massive repartitioning of the entire system. Selecting and utilizing appropriate partition keys is an art in and of itself.

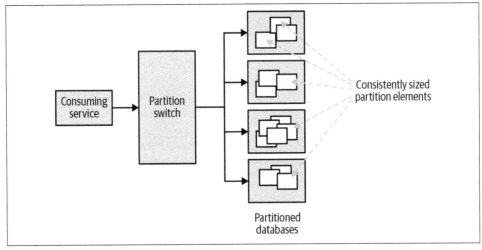

Figure 4-3. Example of consistently sized partitioned elements

Timely Handling of Growing Pains

Most modern applications experience growth in their traffic requirements, in the size and complexity of the applications themselves, and in the number of people working on the applications. Often, we ignore these growing pains, waiting until the pain reaches a certain threshold before we attempt to deal with it. However, by that point, it is usually too late. The pain has reached a serious level, and many easy techniques to help reduce it are no longer available for you to use.

If we don't think about how our application may grow while we are architecting the application before it scales, we will lock ourselves into architectural decisions that can block our ability to scale as our business requires.

Instead, while designing and architecting your new application and changes to your existing applications, consider how those changes will be impacted by potential scale changes in the future. How much room to scale have you built in? What is the first scalability wall you will run into? What happens when you reach that wall? How can you respond and remove the barrier without requiring a major rearchitecture of the application?

By thinking about how your application will grow long before it grows to those painful levels, you can preempt many problems and build and improve your applications so that they can handle these growing pains safely and securely.

CHAPTER 5

Dealing with Service Failures

One of the vulnerabilities in building a large microservice-based application is dealing with service failures. The more services you have, the greater the likelihood of a service failing, and the larger the number of other services that are dependent on the failed service. How can you deal with these service failures without adding instability to your application? In this chapter, we will discuss some techniques to deal with service failures.

Cascading Service Failures

Consider a service that you own. It has several dependencies, and several services depend on it. Figure 5-1 illustrates the service "Our Service" with multiple dependencies (Service A, Service B, and Service C) and several services that depend on it (Consumer 1 and Consumer 2). Our service is dependent on three services, and our service is depended on by two services.

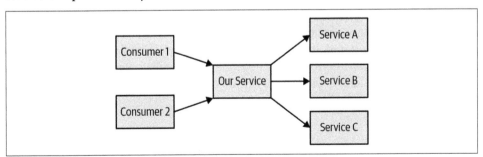

Figure 5-1. Our Service and its dependencies and consumers

What happens if one of our dependencies fails? Figure 5-2 shows Service A failing.

Unless you are careful, Service A failing can cause "Our Service" to also fail, since it has a dependency on Service A.

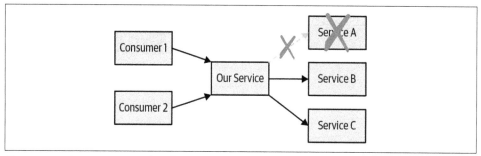

Figure 5-2. Our Service with a failed dependency

Now if "Our Service" fails, this failure can cause Consumer 1 and Consumer 2 to fail. The error can cascade, causing many more services to fail, as shown in Figure 5-3.

A single service failure in your system can, if unchecked, cause serious problems to your entire application.

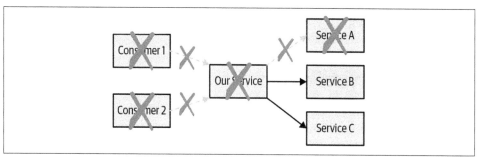

Figure 5-3. Cascading failure

What can you do to prevent cascading failures from occurring? There are times when you can do nothing—a service error in a dependency will cause you (and other dependent services) to fail, because of the high level of dependency required. Sometimes your service can't do its job if a dependency has failed. But that isn't always the case. In fact, often there is plenty you can do to salvage your service's actions for the case in which a dependent service fails.

Responding to a Service Failure

When a service you depend on fails, how should you respond? As a service developer, your response to a dependency failure must be:

- Predictable
- Understandable
- Reasonable for the situation

Let's look at each of these.

Predictable Response

Having a predictable response is an important aspect for services to be able to depend on other services. You must provide a predictable response given a specific set of circumstances and requests. This is critical to preventing the previously described cascading service failures from affecting every aspect of your application. Even a small failure in such an environment can cascade and grow into a large problem if you are not careful.

As such, if one of your downstream dependencies fails, you still have a responsibility to generate a predictable response. Now that predictable response might be an error message. That is an acceptable response, as long as there is an appropriate error mechanism included in your API to allow generating such an error response.

An error response is not the same as an unpredictable response. An unpredictable response is a response that is not expected by the services you are serving. An error response is a valid response stating that you were not able to perform the specified request. They are two different things.

If your service is asked to perform the operation "3 + 5," it is expected to return a number, specifically the number "8." This is a predictable response. If your service is asked to perform the operation "5 / 0," a predictable response would be "Not a Number," or "Error, invalid request." These are predictable responses. An unpredictable response would be if you returned "50000000000" once and "38393384384337" another time (sometimes described as garbage in, garbage out).

A garbage in, garbage out response is not a predictable response. A predictable response to garbage in would be "invalid request."

Your upstream dependencies expect you to provide a predictable response. Don't output garbage if you've been given garbage as input. If you provide an unpredictable response to an unpredictable reaction from a downstream service, you just propagate the unpredictable nature up the value chain. Sooner or later, that unpredictable reaction will be visible to your customers, which will affect your business. Or worse, the unpredictable response injects invalid data into your business processes, which makes your business processes inconsistent and invalid. This can affect your business analytics as well as promote a negative customer experience.

As much as possible, even if your dependencies fail or act unpredictably, it is important that you do not propagate that unpredictability upward to those who depend on you.

 A predictable response really means a planned response. Don't think, "Well, if a dependency fails, I can't do anything, so I might just as well fail too." If everything else is failing, you should instead proactively figure out what a reasonable response would be to the situation. Then detect the situation and perform the expected response.

Understandable Response

Understandable means that you have an agreed-upon format and structure for your responses with your upstream processes. This constitutes a contract between you and your upstream services. Your response must fit within the bounds of that contract, even if you have misbehaving dependencies. It is never acceptable for you to violate your API contract with your consumers just because a dependency violated its API contract with you. Instead, make sure your contracted interface provides enough support to cover all contingencies of action on your part, including that of failed dependencies.

Reasonable Response

Your response should be indicative of what is actually happening with your service. When asked "What is 3 + 5?" your service should return an acceptable answer even if dependencies are failing. It might be acceptable to return "Sorry, I couldn't calculate that result," or "Please try again later," but it should not return "red" as the answer.

This sounds obvious, but you'd be surprised by the number of times an unreasonable response can cause problems. Imagine, for instance, that a service wants to get a list of all accounts that are expired and ready to be deleted. As illustrated in Figure 5-4, you might call an "expired account" service (which will return a list of accounts to be deleted), and then go out and delete all the accounts in the list.

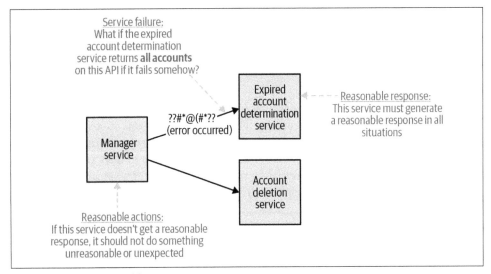

Figure 5-4. Unreasonable API response

If the "expired account" service runs into a problem and cannot calculate a valid response, it should return "None," or "I'm sorry, I can't do that right now." Imagine the problems it would cause if, instead of returning a reasonable response, it returned a list of all accounts in the system? In this case, the "manager service" would go ahead and try and delete all accounts in the system, which is almost certainly the wrong thing to do, and the results would be devastating if suddenly all the accounts in your application were deleted.

Determining Failures

Now that we know how to respond to failures, let's discuss how to determine when a dependency is failing in the first place. How do you determine when a dependency is failing? It depends on the failure mode. Here are some example failure modes that are important to consider, ordered from easiest to detect to hardest to detect:

Garbled response
    The response was not understandable. It was "garbage" data in an unrecognizable format. This might indicate that the response is in the wrong format, or the format might have syntax errors in it.

Response indicated a fatal error occurred
    The response was understandable. It indicated that a serious error occurred processing the request. This is usually not a failure of the network communications layer but of the service itself. It could also be caused by the request sent to the service not being understandable.

Response was understandable, but returned results were not what was expected
> The response was understandable. It indicated that the operation was performed successfully without serious errors, but the data returned did not match what was expected to be returned.

Result was out of expected bounds
> The response was understandable. It indicated that the operation was performed successfully without serious errors. The data returned was in a reasonable and expected format, but the data itself was not within expected bounds. For example, consider a service call that is requesting the number of days since the first of the year. What happens if it returns a number such as 843? That would be a result that is understandable, parsable, did not fail, but is clearly not within the expected bounds.

Response did not arrive
> The request was sent, but no response ever arrived from the service. This could happen as a result of a network communications problem, a service problem, or a service outage.

Response was slow in arriving
> The request was sent, and the response was received. The response was valuable and useful, and within expected bounds. However, the response came much later than expected. This is often an indication that the service or network is overloaded, or that some other resource allocation issue exists.

When you receive a response that is garbled, you instantly know the response is not usable and can take appropriate action. An understandable response that did not match the needed results can be a bit more challenging to detect, and the appropriate action to take can be tougher to determine, but it is still reasonable to do so.

A response that never arrives is difficult to detect in a way that allows you to perform an appropriate action with the result. If all you are going to do is generate an error response to your consumer, a simple timeout on your dependency may suffice in catching the missing response.

A Better Approach to Catching Responses That Never Arrive

A timeout doesn't always work, however. For instance, what do you do if a service usually takes 50 ms to respond, but the variation can cause the response to come as quickly as 10 ms, or to take as long as 500 ms? What do you set your timeout to? An obvious answer is something greater than 500 ms. But what if your contracted response time to the consumer of your service is <150 ms? Obviously, a simple timeout of 500 ms isn't reasonable, as that is effectively the same as you simply passing your dependency error on to your consumer. This violates the predictable and understandable tests.

How can you resolve this issue? One potential answer is to use a circuit breaker pattern. This coding pattern involves your service keeping track of calls to your dependency and how many of them succeed versus how many fail (or timeout). If a certain threshold of failures is reached, the circuit breaker "breaks" and causes your service to assume your dependency is down and stop sending requests or expecting responses from the service. This allows your service to immediately detect the failure and take appropriate action, which can save your upstream latency SLAs.

You can then periodically check your dependency by sending a request to it that is known to fail. If it begins to succeed again (above a predefined threshold), the circuit breaker is "reset" and your service can resume using the dependency again.

A response that comes in slow from a service (versus never coming in) is perhaps the most difficult to detect. The problem becomes determining how slow is too slow. This can be a tough question, and simply using basic timeouts (with or without circuit breakers) is usually insufficient to reasonably handle the situation, because a slow response can "sometimes" be fast enough, generating seemingly erratic results. Remember, predictability of response is an important characteristic for your service, and a dependency that fails unpredictably (because of slow responses and bad timeouts) will hurt your ability to create a predictable response to your dependencies.

Greater Sophistication in Detecting Slow Dependencies

A more sophisticated timeout mechanism, along with circuit breaker and similar patterns, can help with this situation. For instance, perhaps you can create "buckets" for catching the recent performance of calls to a given dependency. Each time you call the dependency, you store this fact into a bucket based on how long the response took to arrive. You keep results in the buckets for a specific period of time only. Then you use these bucket counts to create rules for triggering the circuit breaker. For instance, you could create these rules:

- If you receive "500 requests in one minute that take longer than 150 ms," you trigger the circuit breaker.
- If you receive "50 requests in one minute that take longer than 500 ms," trigger the circuit breaker.
- If you receive "5 requests in one minute that take longer than 1,000 ms," trigger the circuit breaker.

This type of layered technique can catch more serious slowdowns earlier while not ignoring less serious slowdowns.

Appropriate Action

What do you do if an error occurs? That depends on the error. The following are some useful patterns that you can employ for handling errors of various types.

Graceful Degradation

If a service dependency fails, can your service live without the response? Can it continue performing the work it needs to do, just without the response from the failed service? If your service can perform at least a limited portion of what it was expected to do without the response from the failed service, this is an example of graceful degradation.

Graceful degradation is when a service reduces the amount of work it can accomplish as little as possible when it lacks needed results from a failed service.

Reduced Functionality

Imagine that you have a web application that generates an ecommerce website that sells T-shirts. Let's also assume that there is an "image service" that provides URLs for images to be displayed on this website. If the application makes a call to this image service and the service fails, what should the application do? One option would be for the application to continue displaying the requested product to the customer, but without the images of the product (or with a "no image available" message). The web application can continue to operate as an ecommerce store, just with the reduced capability of not being able to display product images.

This is far superior to the ecommerce website failing and returning an error to the user simply because the images are not available.

The preceding sidebar is an example of reduced functionality. It is important for a service (or application) to provide as much value as it can, even if not all the data it normally would need is available to it due to a dependency failure.

Graceful Backoff

There comes a point at which there just aren't enough results available to be useful. The request must simply fail. Instead of generating an error message, can you perform some other action that will provide value to the consumer of your service?

Changing what you need to do in a way that provides some value to the consumer, even if you cannot really complete the request, is an example of *graceful backoff*.

Fail as Early as Possible

What if it is not possible for your service to continue to operate without the response from the failed service? What if there are no reduced functionality or graceful backoff options that make sense? Without the response from the failed service, you can't do anything reasonable. In this case, you might just need to fail the request.

If you have determined that there is nothing you can do to save a request from failing, it is important that you fail the request as soon as possible. Do not go about doing other actions or tasks that are part of the original request after you know the request will fail.

A corollary to this rule is to perform as many checks on an inbound request as possible and as early as possible to ensure that, when you move forward, there is a good chance that the request will succeed.

In the preceding sidebar, because you know that all divisions by zero will always fail, simply check the data that is passed into the request. If the divisor is zero, return an error immediately. There is no reason to attempt the calculation.

Why should you fail as early as possible? There are a few reasons:

Resource conservation

If a request will fail, any work you do before you determine that the request will fail is wasted work. If that work involves making many calls to dependent services, you could waste significant resources, only to get an error.

Responsiveness

The sooner you determine a request will fail, the sooner you can give that result to the requester. This lets the requester move on and make other decisions more quickly.

Error complexity

Sometimes, if you let a failing request move forward, the way it fails might be a more complex situation that is more difficult to diagnose or is more evasive. For instance, consider the "3 / 0" example. You can determine immediately that the calculation will fail and can return that. If you instead go ahead and perform the calculation, the error will occur, but perhaps in a more complicated manner—for example, depending on the algorithm you use to do the division, you could get caught in an infinite loop that ends only when a timeout occurs.

Thus, instead of getting an error such as a "divide by zero" error, you would wait a very long time and get an "operation timeout" error. Which error would be more useful in diagnosing the problem?

Customer-Caused Problems

It is especially important to fail as early as possible in cases that involve invalid input coming from the consumer of your service. If you know that there are limits to what your service can do reasonably, check for those limits as early as possible.

A Real-World Resource Wasting

At a company I once worked with, there was an account service that was having performance problems. The service began slowing down and slowing down until it was mostly unusable.

After digging into the problem, we discovered that someone had sent the account service a bad request. Someone had asked the account service to get a list of 100,000 customer accounts, with all the account details.

Now, there is no legitimate business use case for this to have happened (in this context), so the request itself was obviously an invalid request. The value 100,000 was way out of the range of rational numbers to provide as input to this request.

However, the account service dutifully attempted to process the request...and processed...and processed...and processed...

The service eventually failed because it did not have enough resources to complete such a large request. It stopped after processing a few thousand accounts and returned a simple error message.

The calling service, the one that generated the invalid request, saw the failure message and decided that it should just retry the request. And retry. And retry. And retry.

The account service repeatedly processed thousands of accounts only to have those results thrown away in a failure message. But it did this over and over and over again.

The repeated failed requests consumed large quantities of available resources. It consumed so many resources that legitimate requests to the service began to back up, and eventually to fail.

In the "A Real-World Resource Wasting" example, a simple check early on in the account service's processing of the request (such as a check to ensure that the requested number of accounts was of a reasonable size) could have avoided the excessive and ultimately pointless consumption of resources. Additionally, if the error message returned indicated that the error was permanent and caused by an invalid argument, the calling service could have seen the "permanent error" indicator and not attempted retries that it knew would fail.

Provide service limits

A corollary to this story is that you should always provide service limits. If you know your service can't handle retrieving more than, say, 5,000 accounts at a time, state that limit in your service contract and test and fail any request that is outside that limit.

Summary

Garbage in, garbage out is a problematic way of dealing with errors, as it passes responsibility for recognizing a bad result on to other services that may not be able to make effective decisions. Bad data should be detected as early as possible and handled appropriately. Additionally, services should always act in a dependable and understandable manner, even in failure conditions. They should never generate garbage or incomprehensible results.

PART III

Tenet 3. Organization: Scaling Your Organization for Modern Applications

You cannot build modern software unless your organization uses modern processes and procedures. Modern applications require modern organizations.

It doesn't matter how scalable your application is if your development organization isn't structured to support it, or if your organization does not have the right culture to drive higher availability and greater scalability.

Organizing your teams to better support your scalability needs will create a culture that supports your application's scaling needs.

CHAPTER 6

Service Ownership—STOSA

In Chapter 3, we discussed what a service was and how it could be utilized to help take the complexity of an application and divide it among many different development teams, each working on its own code base and supporting its own services. We discussed how to size services and how services should interact.

But we didn't delve deeply into the specifics of what it meant for a team to "own" a service, and why this ownership is important. In this chapter, we will explain what is meant by *service ownership*, and what is necessary for a *Single Team Owned Service Architecture* to work.

Single Team Owned Service Architecture

What is Single Team Owned Service Architecture (STOSA)? STOSA is an important guiding principle for large organizations that have many development teams that own and manage services comprising one or more applications.

What does it mean to have a STOSA application and organization? To be STOSA, you must meet the following criteria:

- You must have an application that is constructed with a service-based architecture.
- There must be multiple development teams responsible for building and maintaining the application.
- Each and every service in your application must be assigned to a development team, who owns that service. Who owns which service should be well documented and readily available to everyone in the organization.
- No service should be assigned to more than one development team.

- Individual development teams may own more than one service.
- Teams are responsible for all aspects of managing the service, from service architecture and design to development, testing, deployment, monitoring, and incident resolution.
- Services have strong boundaries between them, including well-documented APIs.
- The service owns its own data. Data is part of the service. If a service needs to access data stored in a different service, it must use one of the well-documented APIs to access that data.
- Services maintain internal service-level agreements (SLAs) between them that are monitored, with violations reported to the owning team.

A *STOSA-based application* is an application for which all services follow the preceding rules. A *STOSA-based organization* is one in which all service teams follow the preceding rules and all applications are STOSA applications.

In a STOSA-based organization, each team should be of reasonable size (typically between three and eight engineers). If a team is too small, it cannot manage a service effectively. If it's too large, managing the team becomes cumbersome.

Figure 6-1 shows a typical STOSA-based organization managing a STOSA application.

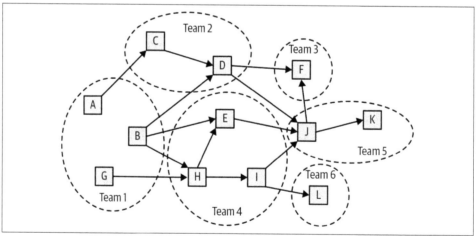

Figure 6-1. STOSA-based organization with a STOSA application

In this diagram, the boxes labeled A through L represent each individual service within the application. The ovals represent development teams that own the enclosed services.

This application contains twelve services managed by five teams. You'll notice that each service is managed by a single team, but several teams manage more than one service. Every service has an owner, and no service has more than one owner.

Clear ownership for every aspect of the application exists. For any part of the application, you can clearly determine who is responsible and who to contact for questions, issues, or changes.

Figure 6-2 shows an example application and organization that are not STOSA-based.

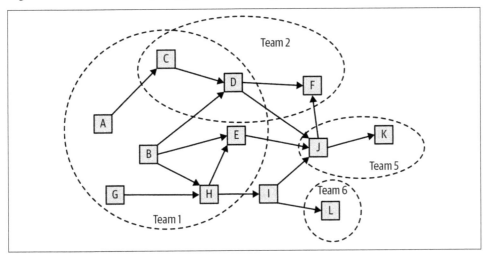

Figure 6-2. Non-STOSA-based organization

You'll notice a couple things. First, Service I does not have any owner. Yet Services C and D are owned and maintained by more than one team.

There is no clear ownership. If you need something done in Service C or Service D, it's not clear who is responsible. If one of those services has a problem, who responds? What happens if you need something done to Service I? Who do you contact? This lack of clear ownership and responsibility makes managing a complex application even more complicated.

Advantages of a STOSA Application and Organization

As applications grow in size, they grow in complexity. A STOSA-based application can grow larger than a non-STOSA-based application and can be managed by a larger development team. As such, it can scale much larger while still maintaining solid, documented, supportable interfaces.

A STOSA-based organization can handle larger and more complicated applications than a non-STOSA-based organization can. This is because STOSA shares the complexity of a system across multiple development teams effectively and efficiently, while maintaining clear ownership and lines of responsibility.

What Does It Mean to "Own" a Service?

In a STOSA organization, the team that owns a service is ultimately 100% responsible for all aspects of that service. That team might depend on other teams for assistance (such as an operations team for hardware), but ultimately the owning team is responsible for the service.

This includes the following responsibilities:

API design
The design, implementation, testing, and version management of all APIs, internal and external, that the service exposes.

Service development
The design, implementation, and testing of the service's business logic and business responsibilities.

Data
The management of all data the service owns and maintains, its representation and schema, access patterns, and lifecycle.

Deployments
The process of determining when and if a service update is required, and the deployment of new software to the service, including verification and rollback of all service nodes and the availability of the service during the deployment.

Deployment windows
When it is safe and when it is not safe to deploy. This includes enforcing company- and product-wide blackouts as well as service-specific windows.

Production infrastructure changes
All production infrastructure changes needed by the service (such as load balancer settings and system tuning).

Environments
Managing the production environment, along with all development, staging, and pre-production deployment environments for the service.

Service SLAs
Negotiating, setting, and monitoring SLAs, along with the responsibility of keeping the service operating within those SLAs.

Monitoring
>   Ensuring that monitoring is set up and managed for all appropriate aspects of the service, including monitoring service SLAs, and also reviewing the monitoring on a regular and consistent basis.

Incident response
>   Ensuring that notifications are generated when the system begins to function out of specification. Providing on-call rotation and notification management, as necessary, to make sure someone from the team is available to handle incidents. Handling incidents within prescribed SLA boundaries for incident responsiveness.

Reporting
>   Internal reporting to other teams (consumers and dependencies) as well as management reporting on the operational health of the service.

Often, some of these aspects are not handled directly by the owning team but are the responsibility of a shared infrastructure, tools, operations, or platform engineering team. Even in those cases in which aspects are handled by other core teams, however, it is ultimately the service owner's responsibility to make sure the activities are handled to the level required to meet their SLAs and customer expectations.

The following items often are handled by shared teams on behalf of the owning team:

Servers/hardware
>   All hardware and infrastructure needed to run the hardware for production and all supporting environments. This is often provided by an operations team, or by a cloud provider, or both.

Tooling
>   Various tooling required by the owning team is often centrally owned and managed. This can include deployment tools, compiling and code management tools, monitoring tools, on-call and incident response tools, and reporting tools.

Databases
>   The hardware and database applications that store the data used by the service are often managed by a central team. However, the data itself, the data schema, and the use of the data are always managed by the owning team.

Figure 6-3 shows a typical organization hierarchy for a STOSA-based organization. Essentially, all development teams that are service-owning teams are peers, organizationally. They are all supported uniformly by a series of supporting teams, including operations, tooling, databases, and other similar teams. All of these may or may not also sit on top of other core teams that have universal responsibility for the organization but not for individual services. These can include teams such as an architectural guidance team or a program management team.

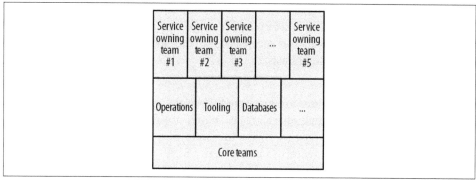

Figure 6-3. STOSA-based organization hierarchy

Service-owning teams in a STOSA organization are the teams that are ultimately responsible for all aspects of the services they own. A service-owning team might depend on the core and support teams, but it is ultimately responsible for ensuring that all issues are dealt with and that the service is operating properly.

For example, let's assume that a service fails because a deployment went bad due to a failure in the core deployment tool. The service failure is the responsibility of the service-owning team. That team may have issues or concerns with the tooling team that it needs to deal with, but ultimately the service-owning team is the one responsible for the failure. It cannot simply say "it was the tooling team's fault." Ultimately, even if that were true, it was the service that failed, and hence the service-owning team is responsible.

With strong ownership of results also comes strong ownership of decision making affecting your service. Typically, a service-owning team is given a set of requirements it needs to implement, but the details of how those requirements are implemented are the team's responsibility. The team might have system-wide compliance requirements it needs to conform to (such as architecture guidelines or rules, tooling that must be used, language and hardware selection restrictions, or industry-specific regulatory requirements), but these ultimately are part of the service requirements given to the owning team.

Beyond these requirements, all design details and decisions are the responsibility of the owning team.

Ultimately, the owning team is making a commitment to achieve an expected set of results and maintain an appropriate set of SLAs.

Using Core Teams and Services

Often in a strong STOSA-based organization, service teams may choose not to make use of a standard shared core and support capabilities. As an example, they may support their own database rather than using a database provided and supported by a centralized database team. Or they could decide to use their own cloud provider rather than the cloud provider supported by the operations team.

As long as a service team meets its specified requirements, it does not necessarily need to be forced to use these common infrastructure components. Of course, there are advantages for the service team in utilizing standard, shared capabilities. If the team chooses not to use these supported shared capabilities, it may in fact generate additional support headaches for itself. The key, though, is that this decision is the decision of the service team to make—and it has to live with the repercussions.

One advantage of this model is it gives motivation and responsibility to the core teams to treat the service teams as real customers…customers that can go somewhere else if they don't provide the capabilities they require. This can provide strong motivation for a centralized team to provide higher quality offerings to the service teams.

Your organization does not have to do this to support STOSA, and in fact your organization may put in service requirements that require the use of core infrastructure components. But in general, the greater the flexibility given to the service teams, the greater the ingenuity and ultimately the better the services that are produced.

As your organization grows and scales, there will be a natural tendency toward accepting these standardized core platform teams by the individual service teams. In fact, in a large, highly scaled organization, there may be little difference between service teams that are "forced" to use common platforms and those that "choose" to because it's the only way for them to meet their specified requirements. The more you can make this a choice, whether real or perceived, the better buy-in you'll have within your organization in general.

Summary

STOSA is an important model for determining how services should be owned and managed by individual development teams. It describes a model for an organization culture that makes building and maintaining services a scalable practice. In the remaining chapters in Part II, we'll continue discussing service ownership as we focus on service interactions and the interfaces between services.

CHAPTER 7

Service Tiers

Working with large, complex applications with many services can cause availability issues. A failure of a single service can cause services that depend on it to fail. This can cause a cascade effect that results in your entire application failing. This is especially egregious when the service that failed is not itself a mission-critical service but it causes mission-critical services to fail.

Service tiers are labels associated with a service that indicate the criticalness of that service to the operation of your business. Service tiers allow you to manage your application complexity and understand the importance of individual application services in a distributed and organized manner.

Application Complexity

As illustrated in Figure 7-1, sometimes the smallest and least significant of services can fail.

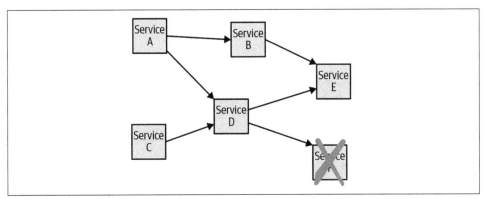

Figure 7-1. A single service failure...

This can cause your entire application to go down, as illustrated in Figure 7-2.

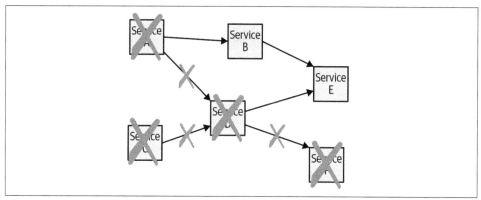

Figure 7-2. ...can cause a cascade failure

There are many ways to prevent dependent services from failing, and we discuss many of these in Chapter 5. However, adding resiliency between services also adds complexity and cost, and sometimes it is not needed. Looking at Figure 7-3, what happens if Service D is not critical to the running of Service A? Why should Service A fail simply because Service D has failed?

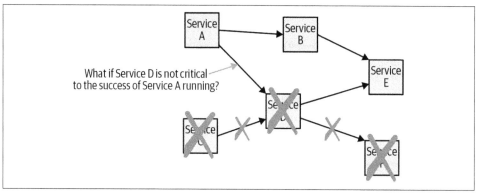

Figure 7-3. What if Service D is not critical?

How do you know when a service dependency link is critical and when it isn't? Service tiers are one way to help manage this.

What Are Service Tiers?

A service tier is simply a label associated with a service that indicates how critical the service is to the operation of your business. Service tiers let you distinguish between services that are mission critical and those that are useful and helpful but not essential.

By comparing service tier levels of dependent services, you can determine which service dependencies are most sensitive and which are less important.

Assigning Service Tier Labels to Services

All services in your system, no matter how big or how small, should be assigned a service tier. The following sections outline a scale to get you started (you can make adjustments to these recommendations as necessary to accommodate your particular business needs).

Tier 1

Tier 1 services are the most critical services in your system. A service is considered Tier 1 if a failure of that service will result in a significant impact on customers or on the company's bottom line.

The following are some examples of Tier 1 services:

Login service
> If customers can't log in to your application, then your application is unusable to them.

Credit card processor
> If customers can't use their credit cards, they can't complete orders and your business can't make money.

Permission service
> Not all customers have the same access to the same capabilities. If the permission service is down, customers will lose access to their allowed capabilities.

Order accepting service
> If customers can't check out and complete the processing of their orders, then your business can't make money and customers can't get and use your product.

A Tier 1 service failure is a serious concern to your company.

Tier 2

A Tier 2 service is one that is important to your business but less critical than a Tier 1. A failure in a Tier 2 service can cause a degraded customer experience in a noticeable and meaningful way but does not completely prevent your customer from interacting with your system.

Tier 2 services are also services that affect your backend business processes in significant ways but might not be directly noticeable to your customers.

The following are some examples of Tier 2 services:

Search service
Customers want to be able to search for products and information on your site. Without it, they can still use your site, but with reduced functionality.

Order fulfillment service
Processing your order in the warehouse is important to being able to ship orders to customers, but customers won't notice brief outages in the ability to fulfill orders.

The failure of a Tier 2 service will have a negative customer impact but does not represent a complete system failure.

Tier 3

A Tier 3 service is one whose failure can have minor, unnoticeable, or difficult-to-notice customer impact or has limited effect on your business and systems.

The following are some examples of Tier 3 services:

Customer icon service
A service that displays a customer icon or avatar on a website page. If it is not working, most people probably wouldn't even notice. But if they do, it won't be a major issue.

Recommendations service
A recommendations service is a great way to cross-sell product on your site, but if it is not working, customers can still make purchases and you can still fulfill those orders.

Message of the day service
Often we want to show all customers a message at the top of the page when they first arrive on our site. If we can't do that, customers may miss out on a sale, but they may not even know that they are missing anything.

Customers may or may not even notice that a Tier 3 service is failing.

Tier 4

A Tier 4 service is a service that, when it fails, causes no significant effect on the customer experience and does not significantly affect the customer's business or finances.

The following are some examples of Tier 4 services:

Sales report generator service
A service that generates a weekly sales report. Although the sales report is important, a short-term failure of the generator service will not have a significant impact.

Marketing email sending service

A service that generates emails sent regularly to your customers. If this service is down for a period of time, email generation might be delayed, but that will typically not significantly affect you or your customers.

Example: Online Store

Figure 7-4 is an example application composed of many services. It is designed for operating an online store. Each service has a label indicating the service tier assigned to the service.

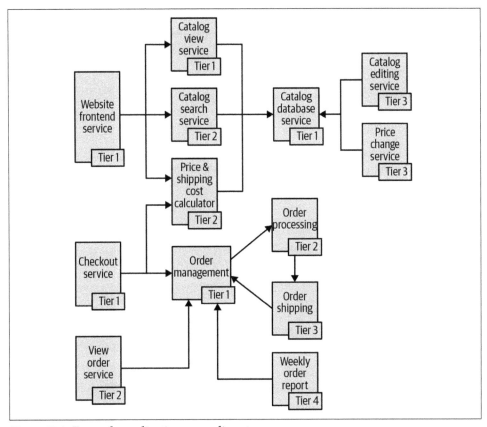

Figure 7-4. Example application: an online store

Look at Figure 7-4 and imagine from the descriptions what the responsibility of each service is. Imagine what the customer experience can or should be when a particular service is malfunctioning. The service tier should be in line with this perceived customer experience.

Here are some example services from this application for you to consider:

Website frontend service (Tier 1)

This is the service that generates and displays the website. It generates the HTML and interacts with the user's browser for the main storefront.

This is a Tier 1 service because without it your entire online store is unavailable to your customers. It passes the Tier 1 test because if it is not available, that has a huge impact on your customers.

Catalog view service (Tier 1)

This service reads the catalog database and sends the appropriate catalog data to the frontend service. It's used to generate the detail pages that show the details of individual products in the database.

This is a Tier 1 service because without it your customers can't view any products online. It passes the Tier 1 test because if it is not available, that has a huge impact on your customers.

Catalog search service (Tier 2)

This service handles search requests from users and returns lists of products that match the search terms.

This is a Tier 2 service because, even though search is an important customer feature to the website, it is possible for customers to browse to products and still use your site without the search bar working. The experience is obviously diminished, but it is still usable.

Catalog database service (Tier 1)

This is the database that stores the catalog itself.

This is a Tier 1 service because without the catalog database, no product can be displayed.

Catalog editing service (Tier 3)

This is the service that your employees use to add new entries to the catalog and update existing entries.

This service is considered a Tier 3 service because it is not mission critical to the ability of customers to successfully complete a purchase. Although not being able to add products to your database will affect your business, it doesn't immediately or directly affect your customers, and a bit of an outage might be acceptable.

Checkout service (Tier 1)

This is the service that displays the checkout process to your customers. Without this service, your customers can't buy products from you.

This is a Tier 1 service, because it has a significant impact on both your customers (they can't buy things) and your business (you can't make money without customers buying things).

Order shipping service (Tier 3)

This is the service that manages the process of boxing and shipping your customers' orders (an obviously simplified example). Without this service, your customers can't receive orders they have placed.

It may seem like this should be a Tier 1 service because shipping orders is a mission-critical aspect of your business, but think of it this way: if you can't ship orders for an hour, what's the impact on your customers? What about your business? In most cases, it would have little to no impact on your customers—a one-hour shipping delay wouldn't affect when customers receive their orders. It would have some effect on your business, because the employees that pack orders might not be able to do their jobs for a while. Because it does not have a significant effect on your business or a significant impact on your customers, a Tier 3 label is appropriate.

Weekly order report (Tier 4)

This is the service that gathers your ordering data and generates weekly business reports to finance and management.

This is a Tier 4 service because it has no impact on customer experience at all. Having a report delayed for a short period of time might affect your business, but likely not significantly.

This example should give you an idea of how you can generate appropriate service tier labels for all your services.

Now that you understand the various tier levels, you should be able to apply appropriate service tier labels to all of the services in your application. Now that our services are labeled, how do we use the labels, and what value do they bring?

Using Service Tiers

After you have assigned service tiers to all of your services, how do you take advantage of these labels in the operation of your services? There are a few ways:

Expectations

What is the expected uptime for the service? What is its reliability? How many problems does it have? How often is it allowed to fail?

Responsiveness

How quickly should you respond to a problem, and what courses of action are available to you in resolving the issue?

Dependencies

What are the service tiers of your dependencies and those who depend on you, and how do these affect your service interactions?

Let's look at each of these.

Expectations

Your service's expectations are an important part of your service to your customers. Service-level agreements (SLAs) are one way to manage these expectations. This is so important that Chapter 8 is entirely dedicated to this topic.

Responsiveness

When a problem occurs in your system, your responsiveness to the issue depends on these two factors:

- The severity of the issue
- The tier of the service that is having the issue

A high-severity problem on a Tier 1 service should be treated as more important than a high-severity problem on a Tier 3 service. That is clear. But if a Tier 1 service has a medium-severity problem, this might need a higher level of responsiveness than a high-severity problem on a Tier 3 service. Figure 7-5 demonstrates this.

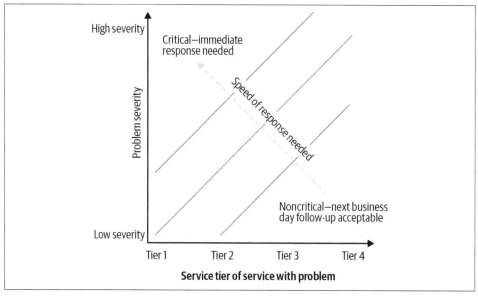

Figure 7-5. Responsiveness for service tier versus problem severity

The higher the severity of the problem, or the higher the importance of the service (lower service tier number), the more critical a quick response to the problem becomes. The parallel lines in Figure 7-5 show lines of similar response importance.

A low- to medium-severity Tier 1 problem would require a similar response to an extremely high-severity Tier 3 problem. A Tier 4 problem almost never requires a critical response.

Furthermore, a low-severity Tier 2 problem would require a similar response to a high-severity Tier 4 problem.

You can use this information to adjust many aspects of your responsiveness. For example, you can use the responsiveness level to determine the following:

- Which types of problems for which services require an immediate notification to be sent
- The expected resolution SLAs
- The escalation path for slow response or slow resolution
- A schedule for when a response should be provided (24 × 7 or business hours only)
- Whether emergency deployment or production changes are warranted
- The SLAs in which your service should perform around availability and responsiveness

Dependencies

If you are building a service, the relationship between the service tier you assign to your service and the service tier of your dependencies is important. Figure 7-6 shows the relationship between your service tier level and that of a service dependency.

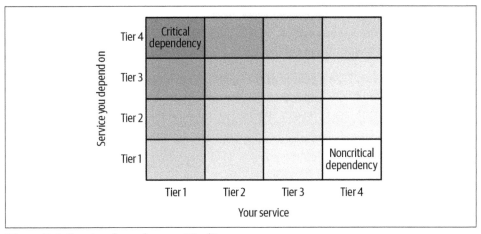

Figure 7-6. Service dependency criticality

If your service is a higher tier (lower number) than your dependent service, your dependency is a critical dependency. If your service is a lower tier (higher number) than your dependent service, your dependency is a noncritical dependency.

Critical dependency

If you've determined that your dependency is critical, it is important that you, as a service developer, deal with failures of your dependency in a way that does not significantly affect your service.

Your service is responsible for performing as much of its capabilities as is possible if a critical dependency fails. This is because the dependency is a lower tier (higher number), which means it likely will not have the same level of availability and reliability as your service requires.

As an example, look at the application shown in Figure 7-4 and focus on the website frontend service, which is a Tier 1 service. When this service tries to display a specific product detail page to a customer, it needs to determine the current price of the product. To do this, it makes calls to the price & shipping cost calculator (PSCC) service to determine the price.

What if the PSCC service (a Tier 2 service) is down? The website frontend service (a Tier 1 service) still must function as best as it can. So what does it need to do?

It needs to gracefully handle failure messages (or lack of response) from the PSCC service. As soon as it determines that the PSCC service is down, it needs to figure out what to do in displaying the product detail page. There are a couple options:

- It could show a cached copy of the price on the page (if it had that available).
- It could show the product detail page but without the current price. Instead, it could show a message such as "Not available," or "Price not currently available," or even "Add to cart to see current price."

The customer can still see pictures of the product, customer reviews, and other product details. Although the experience is degraded, the customer can still complete some very important tasks on your site.

We call this *graceful degradation* (dealing with service failures was covered in greater detail in Chapter 5).

Noncritical dependency

If you've determined that your dependency is noncritical, you can mostly ignore service failures of the dependency.

This is because your dependent service, having a higher tier (lower number), will have higher levels of availability and responsiveness than your service requires.

As an example, consider the online store application illustrated in Figure 7-4, but this time focus on the weekly order report service, which is a Tier 4 service. For it to get the information it needs to generate its report, it makes calls to the order management service, which is a Tier 1 service.

What happens if the order management service is down? What should the weekly order report service do? Well, it's probably reasonable for the weekly order report service to simply fail as well. Given that the order management service is a Tier 1 service, any problems it has will be dealt with very quickly, with a high responsiveness and a high sense of urgency—much higher than would be needed to deal with the failure of the weekly order report service.

As such, the weekly order report service does not need to do anything special to deal with an outage of the order management service, because it is OK for the weekly order report service to simply not operate if the order management service is not available.

Summary

Service tiers provide a convenient way of expressing the criticality of a service to the service's owners, dependencies, and consumers. They provide a way of understanding expectations between services in a manner that is simple to understand and communicate. Simplicity reduces the chance of mistakes occurring, and service tiers provide a simple model for communicating expectations in a manner designed to be easy to understand and easy to utilize.

CHAPTER 8

Service-Level Agreements

Service-level agreements (SLAs) are all about *expectations management*. As discussed in Chapter 7, each service has different expectations around it. Many of these expectations are tied to the service tier of the service, but when we look deeper, the expectations are more specific than that.

SLAs as discussed in this book are not about legal or contractual agreements between a company and its customers; they're agreements between teams and service owners. They provide a mechanism for communicating expectations between services.

SLA Versus SLO

In recent years, the term *SLO*, or service-level objective, has come into common usage. The distinction between SLA and SLO is that an SLA is used to describe a legal commitment to an external customer, while an SLO is used to describe the target for a service metric between teams. Using these definitions, agreements from one service to another such as those discussed in this chapter are more consistent with the term *SLO*. Technically, this is a valid distinction using this latest terminology.

However, I do not agree with this distinction. This is because, from my standpoint, this distinction waters down the importance of service-to-service commitments by using what seems like a less committed term (SLO). The term *SLO* appears to describe a weaker commitment than SLA describes. This is the heart of the problem. In my mind, the performance commitment that is made from one team for one service to another team with another service deserves the same level of importance as a customer's legal commitment. As such, I use the term SLA for customer agreements and for internal service-to-service commitments.

For these reasons, in this book and especially in this chapter, you can safely assume that the terms *SLO* and *SLA* are mostly interchangeable.

In this chapter, we're going to talk about SLAs and their use within the context of both external customers and internal customers. We will talk about SLAs as a method of gaining trust between service teams and how to use SLAs for interteam problem solving.

What Are SLAs?

SLAs are a commitment to provide a given level of reliability and performance. They are used to create a strong contractual relationship between service owners and consumers.

An overnight delivery service, for example, might have an SLA that states it will deliver a package before 9 a.m. the next morning. An airline might have an SLA expressing its ability to deliver checked baggage within 30 minutes after a flight arrives. A power company might have an SLA that states how fast it will fix power outages after a storm.

Customer Expectations

Think back to the previous chapter and consider the online store application illustrated in Figure 7-4. Your customers expect the store to be operating when they want to use it—they expect it to be highly available. They also expect that the site will load fast so that they can use it without delay. Further, they expect the products they want to be available in your store. They expect you to have them in stock and available for shipment. Finally, they expect that when they place an order, the order will show up on their doorstep in a reasonable period of time.

Using "Customer Expectations" example, each of these expectations can be expressed as an SLA:

Availability
> Customers expect the store to be operational when they need it. You can express this as a minimum percentage of time that your store is operational. An example availability SLA might be, "Our store will be available at least 99.4% of the time."

Load time
> Customers expect the web page to load fast—they want the website to appear responsive. There are many ways you can express this, but in the simplest way, it can be expressed as the maximum amount of time a page will take to load—for instance, "Pages will load within 4 seconds 99% of the time" (see "Top Percentile SLAs" on page 100).

Products

Customers expect the products they want to be available in your store. They also expect those products to be in stock and ready for shipment. You might express this as a percentage, such as "A minimum of 80% of the products in our catalog are in stock."

Shipment

Customers expect the products they order to arrive quickly. You might express this as the time from order until the product is shipped, or as the amount of time until a product appears on the customer's doorstep. As an example, "We ship all products within 24 hours."

All of these are examples of SLAs. Although they are all quite different in nature and meaning, they all fundamentally have the same purpose. They express an expectation of your application by your customers.

You can measure the actual performance of each of these things as your application runs and interacts with customers. You might generate charts and graphs that show your measurements over time. But the SLA is the agreed limit at which your service can be considered performing as expected. The chart in Figure 8-1 shows your store's performance on product in stock, which is a measure of the percentage of the products that are in stock at any given point in time.

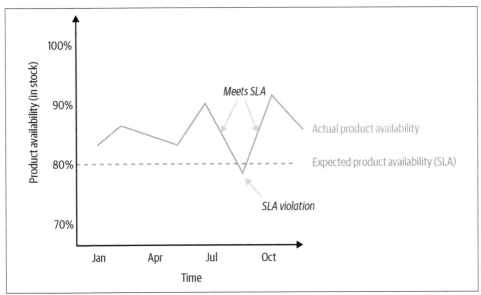

Figure 8-1. Performance compared to SLA

You can see from the chart that your in-stock percentage varies over time. You can also see your SLA line, representing your expected performance of 80%.

Most of the time, your in-stock percentage is above the SLA (we say you are meeting your SLA). However, one time in late summer it dropped below your 80% SLA for a short period of time (we say you have failed your SLA).

External SLAs and Customer Commitments

Sometimes a business has contractual agreements with customers that require it to meet established SLAs, perhaps with financial or other consequences for failing to meet them.

Amazon Web Services, for example, has SLAs with its customers and in some cases provides financial compensation if it fails to meet those SLAs.

For example, with Amazon EC2 instances, if AWS's monthly uptime percentage falls below 99.95%, it gives a service credit of 10% to affected customers. If it falls below 99.0%, AWS gives a service credit of 30%.[1]

Having SLAs for monitoring the ability of your application to perform for your customers can be useful for your internal business uses (making sure you perform as expected for your customers). Or, as AWS does, SLAs may be used for making financial commitments to customers. In either case, the SLA and the way you measure performance against the SLA are identical.

External Versus Internal SLAs

The "Customer Expectations" and "External SLAs and Customer Commitments" examples demonstrate the use of external SLAs. These are SLAs we might specify and monitor describing how our application performs to our customers.

But SLAs can and should be used between individual services within your application. In this way, you can use them as mechanisms for communicating expectations and requirements between the owners and operators of individual services.

Why Are Internal SLAs Important?

Internal SLAs are critically important to the health and maintainability of complex multiservice systems.[2] Why? Well, to put it simply, how can a service meet its commitments to its customers if the services it depends on are not meeting their commitments?[3]

---

1 You can find more details on how AWS calculates this SLA and the credit at *https://aws.amazon.com/ec2/sla*.

2 Or SLOs. This is where the modern distinction between SLAs and SLOs described earlier in this chapter may apply.

3 See Chapter 6 for more information on team-level ownership of services.

How can you provide a 50 ms response to your customer when a service you require gives you a 90 ms response?

How can you provide 99% availability when a service you require provides only 90% availability?

SLAs as trust

SLAs are about building trust in a highly distributed and scalable way. When you trust a dependency can meet its expectations, you can set your own service's expectations with confidence.

Building Trust

Consider the online store application illustrated in Figure 7-4. Imagine you and your team own the price and shipping cost calculator service. Your internal customers are the website frontend service and the checkout service. One of the primary operations they depend on you for is to look up the price of a product given the product number. Because these services use this to generate web pages for display to end customers, they need the price lookup to be fast. Your team makes an agreement to provide the price lookup uniformly within 20 ms of the request.

Now, for you to meet this commitment, you realize you need to have fast access to the catalog database service, which contains the data you need to calculate the price. However, given your 20 ms commitment, you are concerned that the catalog storage service might not be able to provide you the data you need fast enough. The catalog storage service is owned by another team. How can you be sure that team will be able to meet your performance requirements? You have two choices.

The first choice is to contact the owning team and look deeply into how its service works, looking for performance issues and problems, and then analyze the team to make sure you trust it will be able to perform as you need. This, of course, is highly intrusive, very expensive, and not practical for a large organization.

The second choice is to negotiate with the owning team and agree on a performance SLA for its service. Suppose that you work with the team, and it agrees to a 10 ms response. You know that if it can respond that fast, you can meet your own 20 ms guarantee to your customers.

As long as the other team can perform to its SLA, you can perform to your SLA.

You can monitor the team's performance against its SLA over time to see how well it does. If the team consistently meets its SLA, you have trust in your dependency, and you can now focus your energies on your service and what you need to do to ensure that you can continue to meet your 20 ms guarantee to your customers.

SLAs for Problem Diagnosis

SLAs also provide a way of determining where problems exist in a complex system. If a service is experiencing problems, one of the first things to check is whether its dependencies are meeting their SLA expectations. If a dependent service is not meeting its expectations, this becomes a great spot to begin looking to diagnose the problem with your service.

Finding a Problem

Consider the online store application illustrated in Figure 7-4. Imagine that you and your team own the price and shipping cost calculator service, as described in "Building Trust" on page 97.

Now suppose that you receive a call in the middle of the night. Your service has become sluggish in generating price lookups, and it's affecting your company's customers. You check your performance compared to your 20 ms performance guarantee. You find that you are now taking, on average, 500 ms for each lookup. This has substantially slowed your company's storefront, and your customers are dissatisfied.

But what caused the problem? Is there something wrong in your service? Or is it one of your dependencies that is having the problem?

It could be your service is having some problem—perhaps with its hardware, perhaps somewhere else. But before you spend a lot of time trying to figure out what is wrong with your service, you check the performance of your dependencies.

Knowing that your service depends on the catalog storage service and that you have a 10 ms SLA guarantee with the owning team, you check its performance against this SLA. You see that it, too, is having a performance problem. Rather than taking less than 10 ms per call, calls to the catalog storage service are taking over 400 ms. Obviously, that team is experiencing a performance problem. You check and find that its on-call team is already engaged and working on this problem.

Realizing this is likely the cause of your performance problem, you begin tracking the other team's progress toward resolving its problem. This makes more sense than spending valuable time fruitlessly trying to figure out what's wrong with your service.

By having well-defined SLAs with all your service dependencies, you can much more easily track when your service is having a problem or when a dependent service is having a problem.

Performance Measurements for SLAs

There are many measures of performance that services can use, and the specific measures used can and should vary based on the service consumer's and owner's needs and requirements. Here are some example types of performance measures:

Call latency
> This is a measure of how long a service call takes to process a request and return a response. Typically measured in milliseconds or microseconds, it is important for the consumer of a service to know how long it takes for a request to be processed, because that time will be part of the total time the consumer takes to process its request. This is the type of SLA used in the previous section's sidebars.

Traffic volume
> This is a measure of how many requests a service can handle over a period of time. Typically measured in requests/second, a service owner must know how much traffic to expect from a consumer in order to meet its expectations.

Uptime
> This is a measure of how much time a service is expected to be up, healthy, and free of major problems. Typically calculated as a percentage, it is a measure of how available the service has been over a specified period of time (typically a day, month, or year).

Error rates
> This is a measure of how many failures a service generates over a period of time. Typically measured as a percentage, it is normally the number of failed requests divided by the total number of requests processed over a given time period.

Limit SLAs

A *limit SLA* typically specifies an operational limit that is expected to be met. If actual performance is better than this limit, we have *met our SLA*. If actual performance is worse than this limit, we have *failed our SLA*. The limit itself is the value of the SLA.

For example, "call rate must be <1,000 reqs/sec" specifies a limit SLA on the expected traffic volume of a service. If expected traffic volume is less than the specified limit, then the service has met its SLA.

As another example, "service will be operational for at least 99.5% of the time" specifies an availability requirement of a service. If the availability of the service is greater than the specified percentage, then the service has met its SLA.

You can apply a limit SLA to most types of performance measures.

Top Percentile SLAs

Limit SLAs are great when you can measure a value and have a guarantee that the value stays better than that limit at all times. These types of SLAs are great for expressing availability, uptime, and error rates.

Another type of SLA measurement is a *top percentile SLA*. You use it to measure performance of an event when the actual performance of that event typically varies considerably.

Top percentile SLAs are great for measuring metrics such as call latency. The amount of time a request to a service takes to generate a response can vary wildly, and most of the time we don't care whether *every* request can be handled in less than a specific period of time as long as *most* requests are handled in less than a specific period of time.

A top percentile SLA is expressed as a percentage of the total data points that are above/below a specific value. The SLA is usually written like this:

TP<percentage> is less than <value>

Here's an example:

TP90 is less than 20 msec

This can be read as "90% of all requests will take less than 20 ms."

Often, we will calculate the performance of an event, such as the call latency to a service, and express it as an actual top percentile for the service.

As an example, suppose that we have a service that responds to service calls. Over a period of time, we have observed the latencies for these service calls shown in Figure 8-2.

We can chart these values, as shown in Figure 8-3.

Service Call Latency - Actual	
Req Time	**Latency**
T + 1 sec	5 msec
T + 2 sec	10 msec
T + 3 sec	20 msec
T + 4 sec	30 msec
T + 5 sec	15 msec
T + 6 sec	8 msec
T + 7 sec	12 msec
T + 8 sec	45 msec
T + 9 sec	12 msec
T + 10 sec	22 msec
T + 11 sec	4 msec
T + 12 sec	8 msec
T + 13 sec	12 msec
T + 14 sec	15 msec
T + 15 sec	14 msec
T + 16 sec	28 msec
T + 17 sec	21 msec
T + 18 sec	32 msec
T + 19 sec	15 msec
T + 20 sec	22 msec

Figure 8-2. Table of service call latencies

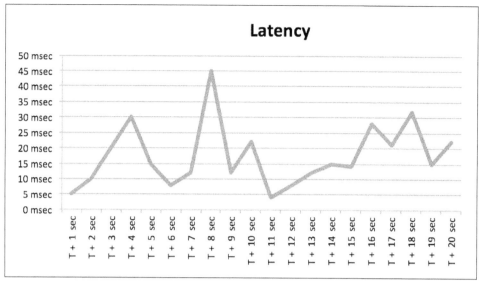

Figure 8-3. Chart of service call latencies

Using this data, we can calculate several *top latency* values for this service:

TP90

This is the value that 90% of the latency values are below. In this example, 90% of the data is 18 data points. Removing the top 2 data points (45 ms and 32 ms) will leave us with 18 data points, the highest value of which is 30 ms. So we can say our TP90 is 30 ms.

TP80

This is the value that 80% of the latency values are below. In this example, that means removing the top four data points: 45, 32, 30, and 28 ms). Among the remaining 16 data points, the highest one is 22 ms. So we can say our TP80 is 22 ms.

Continuing on, here are several TP values representing that data:

TP95 = 32 msec

TP90 = 30 msec

TP80 = 22 msec

TP50 = 14 msec

There are some other occasionally useful values to use:

TPmax = 45 msec (maximum value)

TPmin = 4 msec (minimum value)

TPavg = 18 msec (average value)

The top percentiles can of course change over time. After you have it calculated, you can use a limit SLA to define expectations. For instance, in this example, your service might have the following SLA:

TP90 < 35 msec

If it did, the service would have met its SLA. However, if it had committed to the following SLA:

TP80 < 20 msec

the service would not be meeting its SLA (the current TP80 is 22 ms). So the service would have failed its SLA.

SLA Conditionals

SLAs sometimes are expressed in a way that makes them conditional on another metric. For example, a service might be able to guarantee a specific latency, but only if the call volume stays within a reasonable amount. So an SLA may be expressed as follows:

Call Latency TP90 < 25 msec when Traffic Volume < 250k req/sec

Here, in order to meet our SLA, the TP90 for call latency must be less than 25 ms when traffic volume is below 250k req/sec. If the traffic volume is above that rate, then call latency can be any value.

How Many and Which Internal SLAs?

As you build your service, a question you might ask is, how many internal SLAs should I define for my service?

First, keep the number as low as possible. Understanding the meaning of SLAs and their effect becomes very complicated as the number of SLAs increases.

Ensure that you have covered all critical areas within your service. You should have appropriate SLAs for all major pieces of functionality and especially for the areas that are critical to your business.

You should negotiate your SLAs with the consumers of your services, as an SLA that does not meet a consumer's needs is an irrelevant SLA. However, as much as possible, use the same SLA for all consumers. Your service should have, as much as possible, a single set of SLAs that should meet the needs of all your consumers. Having a set of SLAs created per-consumer adds significantly to your complexity and doesn't provide any real benefit.

You should only specify SLAs that you can actually monitor and alert on. There is no value in specifying an SLA if you cannot validate whether you are hitting it. Additionally, you care if your service violates the SLA, because this should be a leading indicator of a problem, so make sure you receive an alert when an SLA is being violated.

You might want to monitor and alert on values over and above those that you report as internal SLAs. This data can be useful in finding and managing problems in your service without actually being a committed value to your consumers.

You should build a dashboard that contains all of your SLAs and monitors so that you can see at a glance if you are experiencing any problems, and you should make this dashboard available to all your dependencies so that they can see how well your service is performing.

Additionally, ensure that you have access to the dashboards for all of your dependent services so you can monitor whether they are having problems, which might or might not be affecting your service.

Why Internal SLAs Are Important

Monitoring and using SLAs can quickly become overwhelming, and you can easily become caught up in the minute details of SLA monitoring.

Perfect, all-inclusive SLA monitoring is not our goal. Having a number you can use to compare is the goal. Any number is better than no number. The purpose of internal SLAs is not to add up numbers but to provide guidance for you and your dependencies, and to help set expectations between teams appropriately.

Internal SLAs are a critical component in your ability to scale your application size so that more development teams can be utilized in developing and managing your applications. This improves complexity scaling and overall application availability.

SLAs can and should become part of the language you use when talking to other teams.

PART IV

Tenet 4. Risk: Risk Management for Modern Applications

You cannot possibly manage the risk in your system if you cannot identify the risk in your system.

> *...but there are also unknown unknowns—the ones we don't know we don't know. And if one looks throughout the history of our country and other free countries, it is the latter category that tend to be the difficult ones.*
> —Donald Rumsfeld (*https://oreil.ly/EMDXW*)

All complex systems have risk. It is an inevitable part of all systems. It is impossible to remove all risk from a complex system such as a web application. However, examining your risk and determining how much risk is acceptable is important in keeping your system healthy.

This chapter provides an overview of what risk is and how we can identify it. It then introduces a process called *risk management*, which helps us to reduce the effect of risk on our applications.

Let's now revisit the big game example from Chapter 1. Here's a brief synopsis:

> It's Sunday—the day of the big game.
>
> You've invited friends over to watch it on your new TV.
>
> The game is about to start. And...the lights go out and the TV goes dark. The game, for you and your friends, is over.

> You call the power company, and they say, "We're sorry, but we guarantee only 95% availability of our power grid."

The power company in this example is taking a risk. They are risking that the power won't go off during a big game.

They even have the risk quantified (it's 95% likely power will stay on).

The power company knows the types of things that can cause power to go out, such as a power line breaking. As such, to ensure power lines won't break, they will typically:

- Bury them (to protect them from wind)
- Harden them (to reduce the chance a wind storm can blow them down)
- Put in redundant power systems (so one system keeps working even if another is down)

But these strategies have a cost. Is it worthwhile investing in hardened power lines? Is it worth the cost to bury them? Is the cost of the risk worth the investment in reducing the risk? These types of questions are risk management questions, and these are the types of questions we will consider in the rest of this section.

We'll start with describing the fundamentals of risk management, including two very important concepts, likelihood and severity.

Next, we introduce a fundamental tool in tracking risk, and that is the risk matrix. We then talk about methods for risk mitigation, Game Days, and end with ideas for building applications with reduced risk.

CHAPTER 9

Using Risk Management When Architecting for Scale

Risk management involves determining where the risk is within your system, determining which risks must be removed and which can remain, and then mitigating the remaining risks to reduce their likelihood and severity.

When a risk *triggers* (or *occurs*), you or your system suffer a loss. This loss can be data lost by your company or a customer. It can be a lack of availability in your application by your customers. The loss can be invalid or erroneous results. Ultimately, any of these can result in your customers losing trust in your ability to manage their data and their business. This, ultimately, will cost you money.

However, you must weigh this loss against a competing aspect: what is the cost of removing the risk to prevent it from happening?

Ultimately, risk management is balancing the cost of removing a risk with the cost of having the risk occur.

Identify Risk

Your first step in managing risk is creating a list of all known risks, along with their severity and their likelihood of occurring.

We call this list a *risk matrix*, an example of which is shown later in this chapter in Figure 9-1.

Creating the matrix initially involves brainstorming. You can get ideas for what to put in your risk matrix from multiple sources:

- Collective wisdom of the developers
- Known high-support areas
- Known threat vectors or vulnerabilities
- Known areas where the system is incomplete or missing capabilities
- Known poor performance areas
- Known traffic spikes and patterns
- Specific concerns from business owners, support personnel, or users
- Known technical debt in your system

You will likely find that there are obvious entries in the list, but there should also be entries that surprise you. This is good. You want to uncover as many of your risk vulnerabilities as possible, and if some of them don't come as a surprise to you, you probably haven't dug deep enough.

Creating the risk matrix involves assigning prioritized values for the likelihood of a risk occurring and the impact (severity) of the problem that is caused if the risk does occur.

Remove Worst Offenders

After compiling your initial list, review it and identify the risk entries that are your worst unmitigated offenders. How do you know which risks are the worst offenders? Look for risks that occur often or risks that haven't occurred yet but would cause serious problems to your system if they did. The absolute worst offenders are risks that are highly likely to occur or occur often and cause serious harm to your system. "Likelihood Versus Severity" on page 110 discusses the difference between severity and likelihood and how to use this information to help manage your risks. This information will help you find your worst offenders.

Figure 9-1 shows an example risk entry that might be one of our worst offenders, "Frontend fails if user identity service is down."

Once you've identified a few of the top offenders, add items to your roadmap to make sure these are addressed in a timely manner.

Mitigate

For each risk, whether or not it is among the worst offenders, brainstorm if there are things you can do that will either reduce the frequency or likelihood of the risk occurring or reduce the severity of the problem if the risk does occur. These things are called *risk mitigators*.

Risk mitigators can be highly valuable. You are especially looking for mitigators that will reduce the risk (either its severity, its likelihood, or both) yet are simple or inexpensive to implement.

Let's take a look at the risk "Frontend fails if user identity service is down" (Figure 9-1). For this risk, a potential mitigation to consider is to cache user identity information so that some information may be available for the frontend to use even when the user identity service is down.

You can focus on your worst offenders, finding ways to reduce the severity of those risks. But also look at risks that you might not be able to fix any time soon. Finding mitigations that reduce the severity or likelihood of these risks can be nearly as valuable as fixing the risks altogether.

Review Regularly

The risk matrix can quickly become stale if you don't review it regularly. You should review your risk matrix as a team at least quarterly, but perhaps monthly for very active and highly critical systems. Additionally, review it after each incident. Was the incident properly covered by a known risk?

When you review the matrix, first look for new risks that have been recently introduced or newly identified. Add new entries for these risks. Also, remove old entries for items that are no longer risks.

Then look for severity or likelihood changes. Often mitigations were helpful and managed to reduce the severity or likelihood of a risk. Or more knowledge has come forward that makes a risk either more likely to occur or perhaps more severe. This is frequently the case if a risk actually triggered since your last review; you might feel that a risk marked as a low likelihood that actually did occur should perhaps be restated as a risk with a higher likelihood. Now, are there risks that you can remove (fix) by putting them on your roadmap?

Finally, look for new or updated mitigations that you can put into play.

Managing Risk Summary

How do you manage risk in your systems? There are some basic steps to follow to accomplish it:

Identify risk
    First, make a list of all your known risks in your system; this list is called a risk matrix. Prioritize the list.

Remove worst offenders
    Find the biggest offenders in the list, and put a plan together to tackle them.

Mitigate
> For the major risk items that you cannot remove, put together a mitigation plan to reduce the severity of the risk or its likelihood of occurring.

Review regularly
> Review your risk matrix regularly.

Likelihood Versus Severity

It is important to understand the relationship between severity and likelihood. Managing risk involves knowing when you need to be concerned about severity and not likelihood, or vice versa. Understanding the difference is essential in analyzing the seriousness of risks to your system.

We treat all risks as being composed of two components:

Severity
> The cost if the risk happens (for example, what is the impact if customers don't have power?).

Likelihood
> The chance of the risk happening (for example, how likely is a big windstorm?).

Managing risks is managing these two values. You can reduce the severity of a risk or you can reduce the likelihood of it happening. For any given risk, you don't need to do both. But considering both is important to understanding the best path forward in managing risks.

The significance of a risk is the combination of the severity of the risk happening with the likelihood of it happening. To successfully manage risk, you must consider both of these values and how they relate to each other. To reduce risk, you need to reduce at least one of these two values for any given risk.

The best way to understand the difference is by looking at examples of various risks and how their likelihood and severity differ. We'll use the following sidebar throughout the remainder of this chapter to help explain the differences.

Online T-Shirt Store

Let's assume that we are managing an online T-shirt store. This store is your typical online retailer. It provides a listing of T-shirts available; individual pages that show the details of each T-shirt, including pictures of what they look like; and an order processing system that customers can use to purchase and pay for T-shirts that they want shipped to them.

Now let's look at some example risks for this store.

The Top 10 List: Low Likelihood, Low Severity Risk

Using our T-shirt store example, let's assume that the site has a feature that appears on the upper-right side and shows the top 10 best-selling T-shirts. Visitors on the site can see these best sellers and then click to go to and purchase one of them quickly and easily.

Now, what happens if the top 10 list can't be generated for some reason (perhaps due to a service failure)? If it can't be displayed, let's instead assume a static list of T-shirts is displayed, but those shirts displayed aren't necessarily the current top 10 best sellers. This service failure doesn't happen often, because the top 10 list is easy to generate and doesn't tend to have any problems.

What is the risk to our store for having a top 10 list displayed?

Let's look at this risk:

- The *likelihood* of the risk is low because the service that displays the list is apparently quite reliable (I stated the list is easy to generate).
- But if the list does not appear, how severe is the problem? I stated that if the top 10 list doesn't appear, an alternate list is shown. Although not ideal, the impact on our customers is probably quite low, and the impact on our business would likely not be very large, either. As such, the *severity* of this risk is also low.
- This risk is a Low/Low Risk. This means it has a low likelihood and a low severity.

Risks like this are easy to ignore and typically do not need further attention, because they are rare events and the events themselves have very little negative impact.

The Order Database: Low Likelihood, High Severity Risk

Again using our T-shirt store example, let's assume that your list of orders is stored in a typical database. Whenever a customer generates an order, an entry is created in the database. As you process, collect payment on, and ship these orders, you update the data in the database. Later, the data is used to generate financial reports that you can use to show how much business you are doing for purposes such as business planning and tax calculations.

Because the database is important, you run it on high-quality hardware with replicated system components (such as a RAID disk array). You also do regular backups of the data.

However, the database is still a single point of failure. The database contains significant amounts of business-critical data, and your website can't function (you can't even take any orders) if the database is not available. Losing the database would be a big loss.

What is the risk to our store associated with the order processing system's database?

Let's look at this risk:

- The *likelihood* of the failure is quite low, because you are using high-quality, replicated hardware for the database. The database is quite reliable.
- However, the *severity* of a failure in the database would be quite high. This is because if the database does fail, your entire order-processing pipeline will be down, and you risk losing business-critical data.
- This risk is a Low/High Risk. This means it has a low likelihood and a high severity.
- Risks like this are easy to miss because they do not happen very often (likelihood is low). However, they can be very expensive risks if they are ignored because the cost of failure is very high.

Given the high *severity* of this risk, you might want to look at mitigating its severity.

For example, you might want to have a hot database replica standing by, so that you can quickly flip from the broken database to the hot replica. This will let you continue working without significant loss of time or data. Alternatively, you might want to switch to a database technology that distributes data across multiple servers so that you can continue to function even if one of your database servers fails.

Using one of these techniques might very well reduce this risk from a Low/High Risk to a Low/Medium Risk (low likelihood, medium severity) or even a Low/Low Risk (low likelihood, low severity).

Mitigations such as this, which can dramatically reduce the severity of a problem, are discussed further in "Risk Mitigation" on page 122.

Custom Fonts: High Likelihood, Low Severity Risk

Continuing with our T-shirt store example, suppose that you decide to spruce up your site a bit by using custom fonts in all of your text and descriptions. You've found the perfect font to use, and it is provided (and hosted) by a third-party font service provider. To use the font, your customer's web browser downloads it directly from the third-party service provider. If the custom font is not available, a standard system font is used and the page looks like it did previously.

However, you've noticed this font service provider has problems on occasion, much more often than you'd like. When this service provider has a problem, your customers can't use the beautiful custom font.

This happens a lot, unfortunately.

What is the risk to your store of using the beautiful custom font?

Let's look at this risk:

- The *likelihood* of the font not appearing is high, because the service provider is inconsistent and has problems often.
- However, when the problem does occur, your site continues to work—it just doesn't look quite as spruced up as you'd like. Hence, the *severity* of the problem is low.
- Your site might be missing some of its glitz, but it is fully functional without significant problems.
- This risk is a High/Low Risk. This means it has a high likelihood of occurring but a low severity.

Mitigations for this risk involve reducing the *likelihood* of the problem occurring.

You can reduce the likelihood of this problem occurring by working with the third-party provider to improve the availability of the service. Or you can compile a list of backup providers that offer the same font or similar fonts, and switch to them if the first provider doesn't work. These are ways you can reduce the *likelihood* of the problem occurring.

There is not much you can do to reduce the severity, given that it is already quite low.

T-Shirt Photos: High Likelihood, High Severity Risk

Let's now consider the T-shirt images (pictures) that appear on your site as a final example. These are an incredibly important part of your store because people are typically not going to buy T-shirts if they can't see what they look like. If your T-shirt images do not appear, your customers will leave your site and you'll lose orders.

However, the server on which you are hosting your images is flaky. It goes in and out of service and seems to be having problems reading images from its disk. The server is old and needs to be replaced. It fails often and needs to be rebooted regularly. It goes out of service for parts replacement constantly. Yet this is the server used to host your images.

What is the risk of your site becoming unusable because the images are not available?

Let's look at this risk:

- The *likelihood* of the images not displaying is high because the server is flaky and fails often.
- The *severity* of this risk is also high, because if the images aren't available, your customers will go away and not place orders.
- This risk is a High/High Risk. This means it has a high likelihood of occurring (the hardware fails often) and it has a high severity when it does occur (customers won't buy from you).

These types of risks are the most scary. This is a risk that is highly likely to happen, and the problem it introduces is serious to your business.

These are the risks to which you should pay the most attention.

This example might seem obvious, but there likely are many such High/High Risks in your applications. Often, though, these risks might not be obvious until you look closely at your system. This is why risk management is so important.

The Risk Matrix

The first step in managing risk is understanding the risk that is already in your system. Identifying, labeling, and prioritizing your known risks is what the *risk matrix* is all about.

The risk matrix is a critical aspect of managing the risk in your system. It is a table that contains a living view of the state of all the known risks in your system.

Figure 9-1 contains an example risk matrix.

Figure 9-1. A risk matrix (see the following list for details)

Each row in the matrix represents a single quantifiable risk that is present in your system. The columns in the spreadsheet contain the details of that specific risk item.

For each risk item the following information is kept:

Risk ID

This is a unique identifier assigned to the risk. It can be anything, but a unique integer identifier is usually the easiest and is sufficient.[1]

System

This is the name of the system, subsystem, or module that contains the risk. This information is dependent on the specifics of your application, but it could be "FrontEnd," "PrimaryDb," "ServiceA," or something similar.

Owner

The name of an individual (or a team) who owns this risk and is responsible for mitigation plans and resolution plans.

Risk description

This is a summary description of the risk. It should be short enough to be easily scanned and recognized yet long enough to uniquely and accurately identify the risk.

Date identified

The date the risk was identified and added to the matrix.

Likelihood

This identifies the likelihood (low, medium, or high) of the risk occurring. This value is discussed in greater detail in "Likelihood Versus Severity" on page 110. You will use this value to sort your risk matrix to determine which ones you should be the most concerned with and which ones require the most immediate attention.[2]

Severity

This is the severity or impact (low, medium, or high) of the risk occurring. This value is discussed in greater detail in "Likelihood Versus Severity". You will use this value to sort your risk matrix to determine which ones you should be the most concerned with and which ones require the most immediate attention.

Mitigation plan

This column provides a description of any mitigations that can be used, or are being used, to reduce the severity or likelihood of this risk.

---

1 The ID should *not* be the row number in the spreadsheet, however. This is because the rows in the matrix will likely be sorted and new ones added and removed, thus changing the spreadsheet row number for a risk. The Risk ID should be an identifier that does not change for the life of the tracking of the risk.

2 To ease column sorting by the likelihood and severity values, you might want to make them numeric: 1–3 for Low to High, or some other system. A common sorting trick is to use "1-Low," "2-Medium," and "3-High," and then use your spreadsheet program's capabilities to restrict the values allowed to just these three.

Status

This column indicates what the status of the risk is. This is typically something like "active," "mitigated," "fix in progress," or "resolved."

ETA

This is the estimated time for when the final resolution for this risk is planned (if known).

Monitoring

This column indicates whether you are monitoring for this risk to occur, and if so, the steps you've taken to accomplish this. If you are not monitoring the risk, you should indicate why and estimate a date for when you will be able to do so.

Triggered plan

If this risk does occur, what is your plan for dealing with it? The triggered plan is usually a management-level plan rather than an incident-response plan.[3]

Comment

Use this column for any other information about this risk that doesn't fit or doesn't belong in the risk description.

Additionally, other values that are important to your organization can be added as you see fit. For example:

Tracking ID

If you have a bug tracking or roadmap tracking system that contains an entry for this risk, you can put the bug or roadmap tracking ID number in this field.

History

Has this risk already triggered in the past? When? How often?

Scope of the Risk Matrix

At this point, you're probably wondering, "Should I have one risk matrix for the entire company, or one for each team or service?"

This is a good question. One matrix for the entire company is fine for a small company, but it can quickly become unwieldy. One per service affords good visibility at the service level but results in reduced visibility at the company level. Questions such as "Which service has the most significant risk to the company?" become hard to answer.

---

3 Incident-response plans should be readily available to your on-call personnel in your incident playbook or other tools.

I recommend one risk matrix per team. Because decision making on what features or issues to work on and their prioritization is often handled at the team level, it makes sense for the risk matrix to be managed and prioritized at the team level. You can find more information about team-level management in Chapter 6.

Bottom line, you should scope your risk matrices as makes sense for your organization. As such, one risk matrix should be used for each team, group, or organization that typically manages its own decisions about work scoping and prioritization. They may receive input and guidance from upper management, but most work is prioritized and executed at this organizational level.

Creating the Risk Matrix

First, begin with one of the risk matrix templates. We have created some for you in the most popular spreadsheet programs. They are available for download on our website at *www.architectingforscale.com*.

Although you are free to customize the template as needed, for your first risk matrix you should stick as closely as possible to the original template. After you have some experience using the matrix and managing risks, you can customize as you see fit.

The template has an example risk on it to demonstrate how you might use it. Feel free to delete that before continuing.

Brainstorming the list

When you have your template ready, your first step is to brainstorm a list of the risks you feel should be included. Try to include any risk you can think of, not just those that you are concerned about. Don't analyze them during this process—just brain dump all that you can think of.

There are several good sources of insights for this brainstorm:

Dev team
    Have a meeting with your development team. The team members will have an amazingly large number of worries on their mind about their services. Listen to their concerns, and add risk items for each one that comes up.

Support
    Look at your support volume. Are there areas where you are seeing a higher than normal support load? What do your support people say? Do you have support forums you can review? High support areas are a common source of system risks.

Threat vectors
    Think about known threat vectors and security vulnerabilities. Each of these, no matter how big or how important, is a risk to your service.

Feature backlog

Go through your feature backlog. Are there capabilities of your system that are missing and critical to the health of your system? Look especially for monitoring- and maintenance-related backlog items.

Performance

Think about the performance of your system. Are there areas you are aware of that have poor performance?

Business owners

Talk to your business owners. What concerns do they have?

Extended team

Talk to your extended team, including internal users, dependent teams, Q/A staff, and so on. What concerns do they have?

Systems and processes

Do you have documented systems and processes in place? Are there places where necessary documentation for how your application functions is missing, or perhaps is held only in the heads of a few individuals?

Technical debt

Do you have known, specific technical debt in your system? Examples of technical debt include areas of code that are hard to understand or are more complicated or have more moving pieces than are necessary. Areas of known technical debt are almost always risk items.

You will likely find that there are obvious entries in the list, but there should also be entries that surprise you. This is good. You want to uncover as many of your risk vulnerabilities as possible, and if none of them come as a surprise to you, you probably haven't dug deep enough.

Set the likelihood and severity fields

Now, go through the list and set the likelihood and severity fields for each item. Use Low/Medium/High values (or a similar variation) for each of the two fields.

Make sure to keep the concepts of likelihood and severity distinct in your mind. Refer to "Likelihood Versus Severity" on page 110 if necessary. It is often very easy to confuse them as you are working on this step.

It might be helpful to go through and set likelihood first, and then go back and set severity for each item. Remember, it's quite normal for a risk item to be very severe if it occurs, but almost impossible to occur (or, alternatively, very common to occur but not very important if it does occur). You will end up with items in all combinations of Low, Medium, and High states. This is normal and expected.

However you decide to do this task, you will not end up with a meaningful list if you confuse these two values.

Another brainstorming session with your development team is a great way to accomplish this task. This should be a distinct brainstorming session from the aforementioned session, which identifies the risks. Don't label them at the same time that you identify them.

Risk item details

Now, fill in the other basic details of the risk matrix. This includes things like System, Owner, Date Identified, and Status. Make sure to assign a risk ID to each item (a simple numbering from 1...n is reasonable).

Are you monitoring for this risk? Indicate in the Monitoring field whether you have the ability to be notified if this risk is triggered.

Mitigation plan

Starting with the highest severity items first, begin to put together mitigation plans for each item. Then move on to the highest likelihood items.

A *mitigation plan* is a plan for how you are going to, *now or in the near future*, put in changes that are designed to either reduce the severity of the risk or reduce the likelihood. A mitigation plan is not designed to *remove* the risk—instead, it simply reduces the severity or likelihood.

After you perform the steps indicated in the mitigation plan, it will be expected that the severity or likelihood will reduce, and this mitigation plan will be removed. A new mitigation plan can be introduced, if appropriate.

You do not need a mitigation plan for every item in the matrix. There might be items that clearly must be fixed and cannot be mitigated. Additionally, Low Likelihood/Low Severity items do not need to be mitigated.

Triggered plan

A *triggered plan* is a plan for what you are going to do *if the risk actually occurs*. This can be something as simple as "fix the bug," but it can also be more elaborate. For instance, if a risk occurs, are there tasks you can undertake right then that will reduce the impact? If so, they should be elaborated as part of the triggered plan.

Starting with the items with the highest severity first, begin to put together trigger plans for each item.

Note that the triggered plan should not be seen as a replacement for incident-response documentation, such as playbooks. The risk matrix should *not* be a tool that must be consulted during an incident response. Instead, the matrix (including the triggered plan) should be a tool used by management to determine follow-up actions for the risk occurring.

Using the Risk Matrix for Planning

After your risk matrix is created, it should be consulted during all planning sessions. This includes not only long-range planning sessions with product management but also SCRUM-level planning sessions with your engineers.

During every planning session, the most critical risks should be examined.[4] The following questions should be asked:

- Is this risk worse now than the last time I examined it?
- Should we schedule work during this planning period to remove (fix) risks in our system?
- Should we schedule work during this planning period to mitigate risks in our system and hence reduce their likelihood or severity?

Every planning session should include a review of the risk matrix, and items on the risk matrix (either fixing risks or mitigating risks) should be included in your work prioritization process.

If your team makes use of a tool such as Jira or Pivotal Tracker during your planning sessions, you might want to add items in your tracking tool for the most critical risks. If you do that, you should refer to the Risk ID of the corresponding risk in your tracking tool item, and also add a Tracking ID column to your risk matrix to store the ID of the item from your tracking tool.

Maintaining the Risk Matrix

The biggest challenge with the risk matrix is that it is very easy for the matrix to become stale. Your natural tendency is to create the matrix and then put it into a drawer and forget about it.

If you do not take time to maintain your risk matrix, it will rapidly become out of date and useless.

---

4 The most critical risks are those with the highest likelihood or severity, especially items for which both likelihood and severity are high.

To keep your risk matrix up to date and accurate, you should schedule regular reviews of the matrix with the appropriate stakeholders, including your development team and partners. This can be monthly, but it should not be any less often than quarterly. The exact recurrence cycle depends on your business processes. If you have a planning cycle starting soon, performing a regular review of the matrix before that process begins is ideal.

Risk Matrix Review Attendees

Note that it is useful to change your risk matrix reviewers regularly.

By requiring different individuals to review and comment on your risk matrix, you'll get a fresh perspective, and the review will be less likely to turn into a "same old rut" type of meeting.

During this review, you need to:

Look for new risks

Have there been new risks added to your system or recently identified? Make sure these are captured on the risk matrix.[5]

Remove old risks

Are there risks on the matrix that no longer apply—either because they can't occur anymore or because the underlying cause has been fixed? If so, remove these.

Update likelihood and severity

Look for likelihood and severity changes. Often, recently implemented mitigations were helpful in reducing the likelihood or severity, or additional information has been gathered that will warrant a change in the likelihood or severity status. Make these updates.

Review top risks

Review all the risks that are either high likelihood or high severity (or both). Discuss these specific risks individually and make sure all the information is correct for them. Are there new or updated mitigation plans that can be put in place? What about triggered plans? Are you monitoring the risk? If not, why not? What else can you do to improve your situation with these risks?

---

5 However, we recommend that the moment you believe you have identified a new risk, you add it to the matrix. Don't wait for a review session. You can wait for the review session to update all the data in the risk, but you should document it immediately once discovered.

Review less critical risks

Keep going down the likelihood and severity curve, looking at less critical risks as time permits. You do not have to review every risk every time, but make sure the top risks are all looked at often. In addition, you might want to schedule a session to examine in detail the less critical risks, just so they don't get ignored and to make sure there aren't hidden or missed reasons why they should be ranked higher on your list.

Sharing Your Risk Matrix with Management

You should share your risk matrix with your product management and upper management teams. This can be an effective tool for communicating issues with those not directly involved day to day with your team, and for keeping specific issues on the minds of those that need to know them.

One idea I saw implemented recently occurred before a management offsite meeting. Someone was identified to take all the risk matrices for the entire company and combine them into one giant list for the offsite (a read-only copy). Then only the high likelihood or high severity items were kept; the rest were deleted. This master "High/High" list was then used during the management offsite as a way for discussing overall company risk with their products, as well as a way to level set expectations of what types of things different teams put into their matrices and to learn best practices.

Risk Mitigation

The mitigation column in the risk matrix is used to show what mitigations can be used or are being used to reduce the severity, the likelihood, or both values for a given risk. It is all about taking a High/High Risk and changing it to a High/Medium Risk or a Medium/High Risk.[6] It is not about *fixing* the risk, only mitigating the severity or likelihood of the risk.

There is a basic process that you can follow for mitigating risks. A *mitigation plan* details the steps you are going to take (either immediately or in the near future) in order to reduce the likelihood or severity of the risk.

Risk mitigation is knowing what to do when a problem occurs so that you can reduce the impact of the problem as much as possible. Mitigation is about making sure your application works as well and completely as possible, even when services and resources fail.

---

6 Or lowering any other combination, such as Medium/High to Medium/Medium, or Medium/Low to Low/Low.

Let's look at an example of a mitigation plan. Let's assume that we have a database that is used for an application. Let's further assume that we already run the database on high-quality hardware with replicated components, such as using a RAID disk array, and server-grade redundant hardware. We believe our database is highly stable and highly available. On our risk matrix, we have the risk of a database failure as having a Low likelihood.

However, the database is still a single point of failure. If the database server fails (unlikely though that is), your entire system goes out of service. On our risk matrix, we would list this as a High severity.

This risk is a Low/High Risk, and is very similar to the risk described previously.

What can we do to mitigate this risk? Well, one idea is to add multiple active database read replicates and have them available on hot standby, as shown in Figure 9-2. If our main database server ever fails, having an active database standby ready to go will dramatically reduce the amount of time your system is down while the problem is being fixed. This reduces the severity of the risk, perhaps even making it a Low/Medium Risk.

This is a mitigation plan.

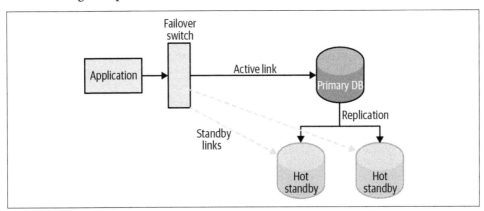

Figure 9-2. Example database hot standby for risk mitigation

What's the difference between risk mitigation and risk management? They are similar but different concepts:

Risk mitigation
> Risk mitigation is about reducing the impact of a risk by either reducing the likelihood that the risk will occur or reducing the severity of the problem if the risk does occur.

Risk management

Risk management is understanding the play between removing risk and mitigating risk. It's knowing whether it is more prudent, timely, and cost effective to remove a risk or to simply reduce the impact of the risk.

Recovery Plans

If a known risk does occur, you must deal with the consequences. You can use a *recovery plan* to create a known set of actions to take to deal with those consequences and repair the problem that the risk introduced.

Recovery plans typically do not impact the likelihood of a risk, just the severity.

A recovery plan is a particular type of risk mitigation that specifically involves reducing the severity of the risk when it does occur. A recovery plan describes what you do if a known risk happens. A recovery plan can describe the following:

- Actions to take to stop the problem as quickly as possible
- Actions to take to implement a workaround to reduce the impact of the problem
- Messages to inform customers of what the problem is and what they can do to reduce the impact on them
- Escalation processes to use and people within the company to inform about the problem (this lets all parts of the company understand and deal with the problem and any fallout)

A good recovery plan is constructed in advance as part of the risk mitigation plan for a given risk, so that when a problem does occur (i.e., a risk is triggered) everyone knows what needs to happen to recover from the problem.

The recovery plan should contain:

- Details of what must be happening that would trigger the recovery plan to be implemented
- The list of actors that need to be involved in implementing the recovery plan
- Step-by-step instructions for implementing the recovery plan, and which actor(s) should execute those steps
- Management and other groups that need to be informed
- Required follow-up that must happen after the problem is resolved

The recovery plan should be stored in a location that is well known to your team—that is, a place where everyone on your team will know to go during a crisis situation. This could be in a support book or an internal support intranet. After a recovery plan is executed, a postmortem of the problem should occur and the recovery plan should be analyzed to determine if any improvements or changes are warranted.

The simple existence of a valid recovery plan for a specific risk item is an example of a valid *risk mitigation* plan that you can use to reduce the severity of a given risk.

Recovery Plan

The replication process described in Figure 9-2 is the beginning of a recovery plan for the risk of catastrophic database failure. However, to be a complete recovery plan, you would also need to include a process for implementing failover, criteria for determining when the failover can occur, an approval process for implementing the failover, and postmortem cleanup after the failover.

Disaster Recovery Plans

A *disaster recovery plan* is an example of a recovery plan that is designed to describe what the company should do if a specific type of disaster hits the company. These types of disasters tend to have a severity of High but will typically have a likelihood of Low.

An example of a disaster that warrants a disaster plan is the loss of one or more data centers for your application (whether that is caused by technical issues, a natural disaster, or a significant security breach).

You can create and manage disaster recovery plans just like recovery plans. The only real difference between a disaster recovery plan and a typical recovery plan is the seriousness of the risk the plan is mitigating and potentially the level of detail and involvement in implementing the plan.

Typically, disaster recovery plans have significantly more visibility within the company and the management and ownership of the company. There may be pre-established, business-specified recovery times required for these types of disasters. But this does not effectively distinguish them from recovery plans.

Improving Our Risk Situation

Risk mitigation is an important process in improving the availability and scalability of our applications by reducing the impact that risk plays in our application. It is a recognition that although removing a risk might not be possible or practical, reducing its impact or severity might very well be possible and often is sufficient to give us the desired level of application health we desire. We talk more about risk mitigation in Chapter 11. When used in conjunction with a risk matrix, risk mitigation plans provide a useful tool to improve the health of your application.

CHAPTER 10

Game Days

A habit that is easy yet dangerous to fall into is to build recovery plans and disaster plans and then shove them in a drawer and ignore them until they are needed.

If you do that, it is almost guaranteed that by the time you need the recovery/disaster plans, they will be incorrect or out of date. In addition, if you do not keep them up to date, you open up the possibility for a number of other problems to be introduced, making the plans impossible or impractical to implement successfully.

As such, you should plan to test your recovery/disaster plans on a regular basis. It should become part of your company culture to regularly test these plans and other risk mitigations.

One model for testing these plans is to run *Game Days*. A Game Day is when you test invoking a specific failure mode into your system and watch to see how your operators and engineers respond to it, including how they implement any recovery/disaster plans. After the Game Day, a postmortem review will uncover issues with your plans and changes that need to be made. These changes will keep your plans fresh and updated and ready to be used when a real problem occurs.

Staging Versus Production Environments

You might be wondering whether you should test recovery plans on a staging environment or on your live production application. This is a tough question and does not have a simple answer. Let's take a closer look at each of these options.

Staging/Test Environments

Testing recovery plans in a staging/test environment is the safest option. Using a staging or test environment allows you to perform invasive testing that would normally disrupt production environments in inappropriate ways. In addition, you can perform those tests without fear of mistakes that could cause production outages. If you decide to use a staging/test environment to test your recovery plan, keep the following information in mind:

- Make sure the staging/test environment is completely independent from your production environment. The testing environment should not depend on any production resources, and the production resources should not depend on any resources from the testing environment. See Figure 10-1.

- Make sure the staging and test environment mimics your production environment as closely as possible. Using a staging/test environment to test your recovery plan can be effective, and you can use these types of environments for testing a wide variety of destructive failure scenarios. However, they cannot guarantee the same results that would occur in a production system.

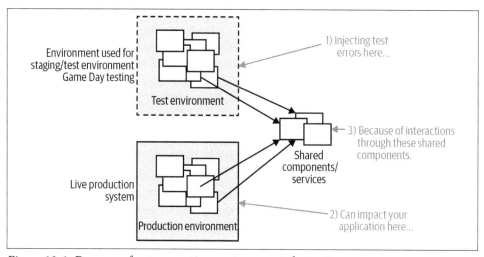

Figure 10-1. Dangers of not separating environments for testing

This is because production systems are almost always scaled to more and larger servers, contain a larger dataset, and manage significantly more traffic in real time.

These differences make certain types of testing in nonproduction environments unuseful.

Ideally, the test environment should be scaled to the same size as your production environment and be seeded with the same data used in your production environment; however, this is usually not financially viable and can be difficult logistically.

If you believe your testing requires a system scaled to the same level as your production environment, you might want to consider production environment testing instead.

Production Environments

Testing risk and recovery plans in a production environment seems illogical. Why would you force a failure mode in production just to make sure that your production systems don't fail? The answer is simple: if you test recovery on your production environment at a time when your team is available and sharp (in other words, not in the middle of the night) and at a time of day that has the least impact on your customers, and you carefully consider the steps your tests will take, you can safely perform testing on your production environments under real-world situations and get valuable data on how your efforts would really perform in real failure conditions.

If you decide to use a production environment to test your recovery plan, keep the following information in mind:

- Be aware of the impact of your injected failure on your live customers.
- Consider the business aspects of the testing. What's the trade-off between adding additional production risk to your customers' use of the system and the reduced long-term risk of learning from the results of those tests?
- Perform the tests at a time when your staff members are at their sharpest (during the workday, when your staff is normally in the office), but also at a time that will minimize impact to your customers (such as at potentially slower traffic times, not during critical time periods like end-of-month or end-of-quarter sales pushes).
- Make sure you have the processes in place that can implement necessary fixes, and roll back failed fixes, quickly and easily.

Concerns with Running Game Days in Production

Game Days on your production environment should be planned and monitored very carefully. Planned appropriately, a production Game Day can be quite revealing of problems within your production environment. Here are some example production Game Days that you could run:

Server failing
   What happens if a single server in your system fails? Try taking one out of service. If your system has a proper amount of redundancy built in, this should not have any impact on your production system. But use the removal as a test of your

systems to detect such a problem, and of your recovery plan for replacing the lost server.

Network partition

What happens if a network outage or partition occurs? Planned carefully, you can simulate a network partition without significantly endangering your production application. But this can be a solid test for the notification and follow-through actions of your system and your teams in responding to the event.

Data center failure

What happens if an entire data center goes down? Planned carefully, your application should be able to handle such an event. How do you respond to such an outage?

Random failures

What happens if you introduce smaller, random errors into your system? Does your application recover from these errors reasonably?

The last item in this list in many ways feels the most threatening. Why? Because you can imagine what will happen when a server goes down or a data center goes down. You probably already have plans in place for dealing with that (if you don't, then you should). But a "random" problem, even if only small in scale, feels like something out of control. It is out of control. But it is these random events that cause you the most problems in building highly available, risk-mitigated systems.

Chaos Monkey

Netflix takes the random failures problem to a new level. The company has a system called *Chaos Monkey* built into its application. This system randomly and regularly introduces random faults into the application, *in the production environment*, with *live running customers*. Exactly what Chaos Monkey does and how it does it are not known to the engineers and operators managing the application. Instead, it is assumed that engineers have put the proper recovery and mitigation processes in place so that the problems that Chaos Monkey introduces can be resolved or worked around without affecting customers at all.

Chaos Monkey runs only during business hours when engineers are around and available to respond to any problems that don't self-correct. The philosophy around Chaos Monkey is to encourage, and actually *require*, the building of highly available, self-reliant services and applications that can survive and recover without human intervention. This is tested during the day when humans are around, with the hope that the problems won't occur at night when the application is busier (more customers) and engineers must be paged into work. It is a novel approach that works well for Netflix.

Chaos Monkey is a great example of a best practice for Game Day testing, and Netflix has done some miraculous things with its Game Day infrastructure.

However, it took significant effort, significant resources, and a significant commitment before Netflix could get to the point where running Chaos Monkey in production could be done in a safe and effective way.

Chaos Monkey should not be your first step into production Game Day testing. But it can be a reasonable goal to work toward if your company has the commitment to making it happen.

Summary

Game Day testing is an important avenue of testing that can help assure your production environment will operate fully at a systemic level. It allows validating your support plans and processes in a safe manner so that when you really need to use them, they will work without issue.

Done properly, Game Day testing can dramatically improve your system availability at scale and reduce your risk of serious problems or failures in your production environment.

CHAPTER 11

Building Systems with Reduced Risk

In Chapter 9, we learned how to mitigate risks that exist within your system and applications. However, there are things you can do to proactively build your applications with a reduced risk profile. This chapter discusses the following techniques:

Technique #1: Introduce Redundancy
Building in redundancy allows you to survive issues that would otherwise cause outages but potentially at the cost of system complexity.

Technique #2: Understand Independence
It's important and useful to know what it means for components to be independent and to understand the (sometimes hidden) dependencies among services, resources, and system components.

Technique #3: Manage Security
Bad actors are an increasingly common cause of availability issues and introduce significant risk to modern applications.[1]

Technique #4: Encourage Simplicity
Complexity is the enemy of stability. The more complex your application, the easier it is for a problem to occur.

Technique #5: Build in Self-Repair
Even when problems do occur, the more automated your repair processes, the less impact a given problem will have on your customers.

---

1 Bad actors are individuals who attempt to harm or compromise a system for illicit purposes.

Technique #6: Standardize on Operational Processes

Variation in the way you do business can introduce risk and ultimately can cause availability issues. Standardized, documented, and repeatable processes decrease the likelihood of manual mistakes causing outages.

This is far from an exhaustive list, but it should at least get you thinking about risk reduction as you build and grow your applications.

Technique #1: Introduce Redundancy

Building in redundancy is an obvious step toward improving the availability and reliability of your application. This inherently reduces your risk profile as well. However, redundancy can add complexity to an application, which can increase the risk to your application. So it is important to control the complexity of the additional redundancy to actually have a measurable improvement to your risk profile.

Here are some examples of "safe" redundancy improvements:

- Design your application so that it can safely run on multiple independent hardware components simultaneously (such as parallel servers or redundant data centers).

- Design your application so that you can run tasks independently. This can help recovery from failed resources without necessarily adding significantly to the complexity of the application.

- Design your application so that you can run tasks asynchronously. This makes it possible for tasks to be queued and executed later without impacting the main application processing.

- Localize state into specific areas. This can reduce the need for state management in other parts of your application. This reduction in the need for state management improves your ability to utilize redundant components.

- Utilize *idempotent interfaces* wherever possible. Idempotent interfaces are interfaces that can be called repeatedly in order to assure an action has taken place, without the need to worry about the implications of the action being executed more than once.

Idempotent interfaces facilitate error recovery by using simple retry mechanisms.

Idempotent Interfaces

An idempotent interface is an interface that can be called multiple times, and only the first call has any effect. Successive or duplicate calls have no effect. Meanwhile, non-idempotent interfaces have an impact each and every time they are called.

The best way to understand this is by example.

The following sidebar describes an idempotent interface. You can call the command "Set the current speed of the car to 35 mph" any number of times. Each time you call it, the car speed is set to 35 mph. No matter how many times you call the interface, the car remains running at 35 mph.

Setting the Speed of a Car Using an Idempotent Interface

Let's assume you have a smart car. The car supports an API that allows you to change the speed of the car. The API provides an interface that allows you to issue the following command:

> **Set the current speed of the car to 35 mph**

Issuing this command causes the car to set its speed to 35 mph.

This next sidebar describes a non-idempotent interface. Every time you call the interface, you change the speed of the car by the specified amount. If you call the interface the correct number of times with the correct values, you can set your car to travel at 35 mph.

Setting the Speed of a Car Using A Non-Idempotent Interface

Let's assume you have another smart car. This car also supports an API that allows you to change the speed of the car. This car, however, has a different interface for the API. This API's interface allows you to issue the following command:

> **Increase the speed of the car by 5 mph**

By calling this API seven times, for example, you can change your speed from zero to 35 mph.

However, every time you call the interface, the car changes speed by the specified amount. If you keep calling the car with the command "increase the speed of the car by 5 mph," the car will keep going faster and faster with each call. In this case, it matters how many times you call the interface, so this is a non-idempotent interface.

With an idempotent interface, a "driver" of this smart car only has to tell the car how fast it *should* be going. If, for some reason, it believes the request to go 35 mph did not make it to the car, it can simply (and safely) resend the request until it is sure the car received it. The driver can then be assured that the car is, in fact, going 35 mph.

With a non-idempotent interface, if a "driver" of the car wants the car to go 35 mph, it sends a series of commands instructing the car to accelerate until it's going 35 mph.

If one or more of those commands fails to make it to the car, the driver needs some other mechanism to determine the current speed of the car and decide whether to reissue an "increase speed" command or not. It cannot simply retry an increase speed command—it must figure out whether it needs to send the command or not. This is a substantially more complicated—and error-prone—procedure.

Using idempotent interfaces lets the driver perform simpler operations that are less error prone than using a non-idempotent interface.

Redundancy Improvements That Increase Complexity

What are some examples of redundancy improvements that increase complexity? In fact, there are many that might seem useful, but their added complexity can cause more harm than good, at least for most applications.

Consider the example of building a parallel implementation of a system so that if one fails, the other one can be used to implement the necessary features. Although this might be necessary for some applications for which extremely high availability is important (such as the Space Shuttle example in Chapter 2), it often is overkill and results in increased complexity as well. Increased complexity means increased risk.

Another example is overtly separated activities. Using a microservice architecture is a great model to improve the quality of your application and hence reduce risk. Chapter 3 contains more information on using services and microservices. However, if taken to an extreme, building your systems into too finely decomposed microservices can result in an overall increase in application complexity, which increases risk.

Technique #2: Understand Independence

Multiple components utilizing shared capabilities or components may present themselves as independent components, but in fact they are all dependent on a common component, as shown in Figure 11-1.

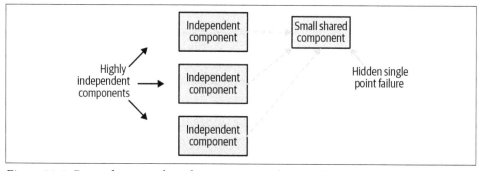

Figure 11-1. Dependency on shared components reduces independence

If these shared components are small or unknown, they can inject single point failures into your system.

Consider an application that is running on five independent servers.

You are using five servers to increase availability and reduce the risk of a single server failure causing your application to become unavailable. Figure 11-2 shows this application.

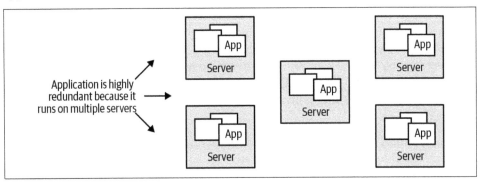

Figure 11-2. Independent servers…

But what happens if those five servers are actually five virtual servers all running on the same hardware server? Or if those servers are running in a single rack? What happens if the power supply to the rack fails? What happens if the shared hardware server fails?

As illustrated in Figure 11-3, your "independent servers" might not be as independent as you think.

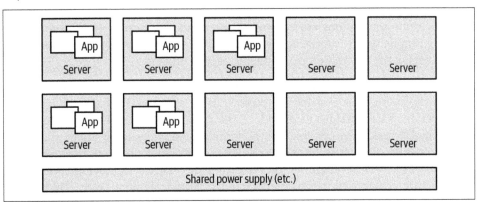

Figure 11-3. …aren't as independent as you think

Technique #3: Manage Security

Bad actors have always been a problem in software systems. Security and security monitoring have always been a part of building systems, even before large-scale web applications came about.

However, web applications have become larger and more complicated, storing larger quantities of data and handling larger quantities of traffic. Combined with a higher usefulness to the data available within these applications, this has led to a huge increase in the number of bad actors attempting to compromise our applications. Compromises by bad actors can be directed at acquiring highly sensitive private data, or they can be directed at bringing down large applications and making them unavailable. Some bad actors do this for monetary gain, while others are simply in it for the thrill. Whatever the motivation, whatever the result, bad actors are becoming a bigger problem.

Web application security is well beyond the purview of this book. However, implementing high-quality security is imperative to both ensuring high availability and mitigating risk for highly scaled applications. The point here is that you should include security aspects of your application in your risk analysis and mitigation, as well as in your application development process. However, the specifics of what that includes are beyond the scope of this book.

Technique #4: Encourage Simplicity

Complexity is the enemy of stability. The more complex a system becomes, the less stable it is. The less stable a system is, the riskier it becomes, and the lower the availability it is likely to have.

Although our applications are becoming larger and significantly more complicated, keeping simplicity in the forefront as you architect and build your application is critical to keeping the application maintainable, secure, and low risk.

One common place where modern software construction principles tend to increase complexity more than perhaps is necessary is in microservice-based architectures. Microservice-based architectures reduce the complexity of individual components substantially, making it possible for the individual services to be easily understood and built using simpler techniques and designs. However, although they reduce the complexity of the individual microservice, they increase the number of independent modules (microservices) necessary to build a large-scale application. By having a larger number of independent modules working together, you increase the interdependence on the modules and increase the overall complexity of the application.

It is important as you build your microservice-based application that you manage the trade-off between simpler individual services and more complex overall system design.

Technique #5: Build in Self-Repair

Building self-righting and self-repairing processes into our applications can reduce the risk of availability outages.

As discussed in Chapter 1, if you strive for 5 nines of availability, you can afford no more than 26 seconds of downtime every month. Even if you strive for only 3 nines of availability, you can afford only 43 minutes of downtime every month. If a failure of a service requires someone to be paged in the middle of the night to find, diagnose, and fix the problem, those 43 minutes are eaten up very quickly. A single outage can result in missing your monthly 3 nines goal. And to maintain 4 nines or 5 nines, you have to be able to fix problems without any human intervention at all.

This is where self-repairing systems come into play. Self-repairing systems sound like high-end, complex systems, but they don't have to be. A self-repairing system can be nothing more than including a load balancer in front of several servers that reroutes a request quickly to a new server if the original server handling a request fails. This is a self-repairing system.

There are many levels of self-repairing systems, ranging from simple to complex. Here are a few examples:

- A "hot standby" database that is kept up to date with the main production database. If the main production database fails or goes offline for any reason, the hot standby automatically picks up the "master" role and begins processing requests.
- A service that retries a request if it gets an error, anticipating that perhaps the original request suffered a transient problem and that the new request will succeed.
- A queuing system that keeps track of pending work so that if a request fails, it can be rescheduled to a new worker later, increasing the likelihood of its completion and avoiding the likelihood of losing track of the work.
- A background process (for example, something like Netflix's Chaos Monkey) that goes around and introduces faults into the system, and then the system is checked to make sure it recovers correctly on its own.
- A service that requests multiple, independently developed and managed services to perform the same calculation. If all services return the same result, the result is used. If one or more independent services return a different result than the

majority, that result is thrown away and the faulty service(s) is shut down for repairs.

These are just some examples. Note that the more involved systems at the end of the list also add much more complexity to the system. Be careful of this. Use self-repairing systems where you can to provide significant improvement in risk reduction for a minimal cost in complexity. But avoid complicated systems and architectures designed for self-repair that provide a level of reliability higher than you really require, at the cost of increasing the risk and failures that the self-repair system itself can introduce.

Technique #6: Standardize on Operational Processes

Humans are involved in our software systems, and humans make mistakes. By using solid operational processes, you can minimize the impact of humans in your system, and reducing access by humans to areas where their interaction is not required will reduce the likelihood of mistakes happening.

Use documented, repeatable processes to reduce one significant aspect of the human involvement problem—human forgetfulness: forgetting steps, executing steps out of order, or making a mistake in the execution of a step.

But documented, repeatable processes reduce only that one significant aspect of the human involvement problem. Humans can introduce other problems. Humans make mistakes, they fat finger the keyboard, they think they know what they are doing when they really don't. They perform unrepeatable actions. They perform unauditable actions. They can perform bad actions in emotional states.

The more you can automate the processes that humans normally perform in your production systems, the fewer mistakes that can be introduced, and the higher the likelihood that the tasks will work.

Rebooting a Server

Suppose that you regularly reboot a server (or series of servers) for a specific purpose (we won't provide commentary on whether this is a good idea operationally).

You could simply have the user log in to the server, become a superuser, and execute the "reboot" command. However, this introduces several problems:

- You now have to give the ability to log in to your production servers to anyone who might need to perform that command. Further, they must have superuser permission to execute the reboot command.

- While someone is logged in as a superuser to the server, they could accidentally execute another command, one that causes the server to fail.

- While someone is logged in as a superuser to the server, they could act as a bad actor and execute something that would intentionally bring harm to the server, such as running `rm -rf /` on Linux.
- You will likely have no record that the action occurred, and no record of who did the reboot and why.

Instead of using the manual process to reboot the server, you could implement an automated process that performs the reboot. In addition to doing the reboot, it could provide the following benefits:

- It would reduce the need to give login credentials to your production servers, eliminating both the likelihood of mistakes as well as the likelihood of bad actors doing bad things.
- It could log all actions taken to perform the reboot.
- It could log who requested the reboot.
- It could validate that the person who requested the reboot has permissions to do the reboot (fine-grained permissions—you could grant access to reboot the server to a group of people without giving them any additional access rights).
- It could make sure that any other necessary actions occur before the server is rebooted—for instance, temporarily removing the server from the load balancer, shutting down the running applications gracefully, and so on.

You can see that by automating this process, you avoid mistakes and provide the ability to have more control over who and how the operation is performed.

Summary

Automated processes are repeatable processes. Repeatable processes are tested processes. Tested processes tend to have fewer errors than ad hoc processes. It truly is that simple.

Reducing risk in systems you are building involves implementing standard techniques that are designed to reduce risk. These techniques are simple but effective ways of reducing risk and hence increasing the availability of your application.

PART V

Tenet 5. Cloud: Utilizing the Cloud

Highly scaled, highly available applications require highly dynamic infrastructures.

As we build and architect highly available, highly scaled web applications, we also have to deal with highly variable load on our applications. From an infrastructure management standpoint, this has traditionally meant the need to overprovision infrastructure resources. If your application needs anywhere from 20 servers to 200 servers depending on the current numbers of users utilizing your application, then you better make sure you always have 200 servers available. In fact, you probably should have 250 servers available, in case your usage estimation was wrong. Failure to do so would mean you could suffer a scaling-related brownout or blackout, and your availability would suffer, and customers would be upset. How many times have you tried to use a website that was very popular at the moment only to find out that the website was unacceptably slow or unresponsive? This is the result of a scaling-related brownout or blackout, and it's the consequence of incorrect resource planning for scale.

As the internet and our use of it matures, our use and expectations of sites go up. The ability to predict scaling needs for these applications becomes harder. Additionally, fewer companies can afford to have overprovisioned resources lying around unused during slow times.

The result? The need for highly dynamic infrastructures that can automatically size themselves appropriately for our scaling and availability needs.

This is one of the most significant features of the public cloud that helps build highly scaled applications. You can very easily provision and retrovision infrastructure dynamically, on the fly, in order to meet your current needs. When your application is in a slow time, you do not need excess infrastructure resources lying around unused, wasting money. And when your application usage exceeds expectations, you can easily add additional resources to meet your current needs.

A well-built application—designed for scale and run on a properly configured dynamic cloud infrastructure—can effectively handle any application scaling needs to almost any level, practically removing the occurrence of brownouts and blackouts during peak usage.

Effectively handling any scaling needs is the goal and the desire, and it is for this reason that utilizing the public cloud is critical in building a highly scalable, highly available, modern application.

The chapters in this part talk about utilizing the cloud in modern, scaled applications.

CHAPTER 12

Getting Started Architecting for Scale with the Cloud

Awareness and knowledge of the cloud has grown significantly in the last several years. It wasn't that long ago that "using the cloud" was something only progressive organizations considered doing or otherwise was limited to startups looking to reduce capital costs in infrastructure utilized.

But it did not take long for enterprises to realize the value of the cloud. Acceptance of the cloud by all but the most conservative enterprises in the last few years has made using the cloud mostly mainstream. Or at least the desire to adopt the cloud is now mostly mainstream.

For many enterprises, though, finding success in the cloud is still a daunting challenge. Too often, organizations set overly high expectations for the benefits of migrating to the cloud while underestimating the amount of work required in the migration itself and the impact the migration has on the culture of their company. An unfortunate result can be a vicious cycle of blame, finger pointing, and grasping for something—anything—that could be considered a victory.

When they find it, organizations may decide they've had enough and stop the migration process before they can take full advantage of the cloud. But by putting off real reform, they won't realize the cost and innovation benefits that drove the cloud migration project in the first place. As migration costs balloon and promised features, functionalities, and applications fail to materialize, companies can end up seeing the cloud as little more than an expensive boondoggle.

Why did this happen? Often, the biggest error comes from thinking about the cloud in the wrong way. Enterprise management tends to think of a cloud migration as a simple "lift-and-shift" operation—simply move existing applications that are running in their own data centers directly to the cloud, with as few changes as possible.

However, real cloud success, at scale, requires much more than lift-and-shift. It demands successfully navigating the world of the dynamic cloud. The dynamic cloud doesn't just facilitate application scaling; it makes the process faster and easier. It also helps development teams respond to changes faster and to implement these changes more quickly. That's not a luxury—it's a necessity to ensure the availability of modern applications that exhibit extreme scaling needs and extremely spiky performance. When you don't know when your customers will use your application, it's hard to predict your static infrastructure needs. A dynamic infrastructure is required to meet the needs of these modern applications without wasting significant resources.

Using the dynamic cloud, however, takes a higher level of commitment to using your cloud resources effectively than does a simple lift-and-shift. That's because after a migration, the type of application and infrastructure visibility that is required changes. Many resources become dynamic, so keeping track of what resources are important for what purposes also becomes dynamic. Additionally, applications now run on an infrastructure outside of a team's direct control, a concept that is foreign to many large enterprises.

Fortunately, becoming proficient in the dynamic cloud does not have to be scary or dangerous. Adopting the cloud can be done safely and effectively, but it is a continual learning experience. Organizations must be willing to learn and adapt cloud offerings to match their needs and expectations with the reality of what the cloud can provide. There is a learning curve of cloud maturity that ranges from simple lift-and-shift to a full architecture rewrite and adoption of the cloud and all of its capabilities. This chapter discusses this cloud maturity curve.

Six Levels of Cloud Maturity

Critically, you can't expect to get there all at once. There are six basic maturity levels that organizations go through during their cloud adoption process:

- Level 1—Experimenting: What is the cloud?
- Level 2—Securing the cloud: Can we trust the cloud?
- Level 3—Enabling servers and SaaS: Lift-and-shift, confirmation the cloud works pretty well
- Level 4—Enabling value-added services: Dynamic cloud becomes a practice
- Level 5—Enabling unique services: Dynamic cloud is deeply ingrained in the culture
- Level 6—Mandating cloud usage: Why do we need our own data centers?

To be successful in moving to the cloud, organizations must realize that this contin-
uum of cloud maturity exists and understand the implications for their actions and
processes. Moving from one level of maturity to the next isn't always easy, it isn't
always fast, and the specific details differ for every organization. Also, organizations
sometimes settle on a level of cloud maturity that's right for their culture but short of
the end goal. That's OK, if that meets the expectations and requirements of their
business.

Level 1: Experimenting with the Cloud

This first tentative step into the cloud relies on safe technologies—technologies that
apply in simple ways to applications and parts of applications that are typically less
mission critical.

Level 1 involves using the cloud for a single, simple piece of an application to test how
cloud services work. Often, the first service used is a storage solution such as Amazon
Simple Storage Service (S3), because it's easy to store some things in the cloud and
avoid addressing the complex processes and systems needed for cloud-based computation, such as cloud-based servers and serverless computation.

This level usually starts as a one-off experiment, where one or more teams conduct
stand-alone migrations. No cloud policies are created at this point; instead it's all
about figuring out exactly what the cloud is.

Level 2: Securing the Cloud

This is a critical evolution point in an organization's cloud culture, as it begins to
involve disciplines throughout the company—legal, finance, security, and so on. Trust
becomes a core question at this point. Can we trust depending on the cloud for our
business success? Can we trust putting our data in the cloud? Do we know how and
where it is appropriate to trust and how to ensure that the cloud is secure enough to
meet our needs?

This is when policies on how the cloud can be used within a company begin to be
formed. The precise nature of these guidelines, from formal policies to ad-hoc "company culture" understandings, doesn't matter that much. What's important is that the
entire company is involved and all stakeholders have input.

Level 3: Using Servers and Applications in the Cloud

The third stage of cloud maturity comes when an organization begins to replace on-
premise servers and other backend resources. These are still simple lift-and-shift
applications, with a basic philosophy of "Let's just move an application to the cloud
and see what happens."

At this level, the goal is to understand how the cloud works for an entire application. This is where the organization begins to enjoy actual advantages from using the cloud, such as reduced cost and increased flexibility.

Enterprises need to be careful here, however. Level 3 can be a danger point. If enterprises attempt to determine the value of using the cloud to run their applications at this stage, they may find they're bearing the costs of the cloud without enjoying the corresponding benefits. That can cause companies to give up and regard their entire cloud effort as a failure. The solution is to use this level not as an end point but as a transition point. Avoid the temptation to stop once you've completed a lift-and-shift and say, "That's enough—we're now in the cloud." It's important to go the next steps and take advantage of the capabilities the cloud provides.

Level 4: Enabling Value-Added Managed Services

Here is where some of the inherent value of the cloud begins to appear. At this level, organizations start to look at cloud managed services, such as managed databases. Managed database services such as Amazon Relational Database Service (RDS), Amazon Aurora, and Microsoft Azure SQL provide database capabilities to applications while requiring less overall management. Rather, you let the cloud provider manage the database. Organizations may also look at services such as Amazon Elasticsearch, Amazon Elastic Beanstalk, and Amazon Elastic Container Service (ECS) to provide managed computation.

As the dynamic cloud starts taking effect here, the cloud's biggest benefits kick in. This is also when companies commit to using the cloud for at least some of their strategic applications and services.

Level 5: Enabling Cloud-Unique Services

Once a company becomes a cloud-enabled organization, it can look to leverage high-value, cloud-specific services. Uniquely available in the cloud, these services are designed specifically for the dynamic cloud. Some examples of services utilized at this level include serverless computing such as AWS Lambda or Microsoft Azure Functions, highly scalable databases such as Amazon DynamoDB, and other generalized services, such as Amazon Simple Queue Service (SQS) and Amazon Simple Notification Service (SNS).

At Level 5, the concept of dynamic cloud becomes embedded in an organization's application development and management processes. Use of these services also begins to tie the enterprise to specific cloud providers. While many cloud providers offer serverless capabilities, each one does so in a slightly different manner. As organizations begin to use these higher-value, cloud-unique services, they become tied not only to the cloud but also to specific cloud providers.

Level 6: Cloud All In

This is the ultimate maturity level of cloud adoption. At this topmost level, organizations begin to require use of the cloud for all new applications and begin to require existing applications to be migrated to the cloud. The usual end goal for customers at this level is to get rid entirely of their own corporate data centers and depend on the cloud for all infrastructure needs.

This level is especially common in cloud-native companies—the needs of legacy applications complicate the ability to be all in on the cloud. It's significantly easier for cloud-native companies to mandate all-cloud-based applications. More established enterprises may choose to retain their legacy data centers. However, more and more traditional enterprises are taking the cloud plunge and abandoning the business of managing their own data centers.

Organization Versus Application Maturity Level

The six cloud computing maturity levels apply to individual applications, organizations, or entire enterprises. But the cloud maturity level of a particular application may be higher or lower than that of the organization as a whole.

For example, early candidates for cloud migration include internal applications, because they present less risk of negatively impacting customers and the business itself. In fact, an internal application may jump to Level 6.

Larger, more complex legacy enterprise applications may be significantly slower in their cloud adoption strategy.

Meanwhile, the overall enterprise itself might still sit at Level 1, 2, or 3 and never make it to Level 6.

This is entirely normal and expected and demonstrates the complexities of cloud adoption in large enterprise organizations.

Cloud Adoption Mistakes

When you adopt the cloud, it's really easy to fall into a few very specific traps that can lead to significant problems in your adoption strategy. These mistakes are often the cause of a failed migration, or at least a perception that the migration was unsuccessful. They can also cause the cost-to-benefit ratio to skew away from the true value of the cloud. Be careful not to fall into any of the following traps as you look at performing your cloud migration.

Trap #1: Not Trusting Cloud Security

One of the biggest misconceptions that companies new to the cloud deal with is the issue of trusting the cloud. This shows up in many different ways, but dealing with security is a main one.

Security is very important to nearly all companies. Moving to the public cloud means taking an application that is safely behind the company's firewall and putting it on a public cloud. The first time you consider doing this, it'll seem scary. Can you trust the cloud to keep your data secure? Is your application safe from attack in such a public environment?

The short answer? Yes.

For the vast majority of companies, your company is probably safer in the hands of a public cloud provider than it is behind your own firewall. Why is that true? Because cloud service providers make a living on trust. They would not be in business if they could not keep their customers' data secure.

Cloud providers invest heavily in building high-quality security teams that spend their time advancing the state of the art in security protocols and procedures. By putting your data in the hands of a reputable public cloud provider, you take advantage of the learnings and best practices created by the leaders in the security field. Unless your company has the same resources to invest in security as the cloud providers do, your company can benefit from these learnings in so many ways.

By using a public cloud provider and taking advantage of all the security offerings it provides, you can actually keep your applications and data safer in the public cloud than you can behind your own firewall.

Trap #2: Performing Cloud Migration via Lift-and-Shift

Early in the process of adopting the cloud, many companies consider moving applications to the cloud by simply taking the application off of servers in their own data center and moving them to servers they've created in the cloud.

This type of migration is called lift-and-shift, and we discussed it earlier in this chapter as a cornerstone of one of the maturity levels of cloud adoption.

While lift-and-shift is a valid way to very quickly get your application out of your data center and into a cloud-based data center, it doesn't do anything to make your application cloud friendly. It doesn't do anything to take advantage of the native value and native characteristics of the cloud. Yes, there are some benefits you can get from a lift-and-shift migration, including the ability to expand to additional data centers simply by launching servers in another region. But that is about where the benefits stop. In fact, the cloud can actually be worse at this type of basic application hosting than your own data centers. Why? Cost.

The cloud can and does provide significant cost benefits for users that take advantage of the dynamic allocation capabilities of cloud resources. But it typically can't compare in cost to the basic, static infrastructure provided by a noncloud data center. When you use the dynamic capabilities of the cloud, you can save money. If you simply lift-and-shift, you typically don't save money and often spend more.

Doing a lift-and-shift can cost you money and time and not give you any of the benefits you were wanting with a cloud migration.

Trap #3: The Lure of Serverless—Depending Too Much on the Hype

It's easy to get caught up in the hype of the cloud, and the latest and greatest cloud service offerings often seem like the solution to all your problems. However, like with any new technology, understanding how and where to apply the technology is critical to successfully using it. This most certainly applies to the newest Function as a Service (FaaS) offerings by cloud providers, such as AWS Lambda and Microsoft Azure Functions.

These offerings promise the ability to provide an execution environment for your software without the need for managing the servers they run on. This "serverless computing" offering is very attractive to companies that are wanting to use the cloud to reduce their infrastructure management costs. But, like all new technologies, FaaS offerings such as Lambda are good for some classes of problems and not good for other classes of problems.

Yet I often hear statements from individuals such as "Lambda will solve my computing infrastructure problems" and "We're moving all of our software to Lambda."

To people thinking that FaaS offerings such as Lambda are a solution to all your problems, I say be careful. AWS Lambda and the equivalent offerings by other cloud providers give a huge advantage to a certain class of computing environments, but they can be overused.

If they are force fit into solving problems they weren't designed to solve, they actually can create more problems for you and your infrastructure management than they solve.

Use them as an important part of your application architecture, but don't depend on them to solve all your computing problems. Use them only where they make sense.

When and How to Use Multiple Clouds

When deciding to move an application to the cloud, you need to consider many factors before choosing a cloud provider. What features do you need? Which cloud is faster? Which one is cheaper? Which one is more reliable?

But here's another question that is being asked more and more often: how many cloud providers should I use?

The seemingly obvious answer is a single provider, but cloud customers cite a number of reasons to use multiple providers. First, some features you might want to use might be available on only one cloud provider, and other features might be only on another cloud provider. Another reason is that utilizing multiple providers instead of being tied to a single provider might offer better negotiation room when dealing with contracts. Yet another reason often cited is reliability—when one cloud provider goes down, the other cloud provider will still be available. Or the reasoning may just be seemingly random...part of your organization prefers one provider and part prefers another provider.

But your answer may or may not be the right one for your organization. Using multiple cloud providers may give you benefits, or it may actually hurt you, when you are doing it for any of the reasons just mentioned.

Let's take a look at what goes into making the best decision for your particular situation.

Defining What We Mean by Multiple Clouds

Before we talk about how many clouds you need, we need some definitions. The actual set of advantages and disadvantages of a multi-cloud arrangement depends greatly on the type of multi-cloud environment you are considering. So let's look at three different types of cloud configurations: joint cloud applications, selective cloud applications, and single cloud applications.

Joint cloud applications

A joint cloud application is when a single application uses two or more cloud providers to provide parallel capabilities. A given application or its services can run on any or all of the supported cloud providers, as shown in Figure 12-1.

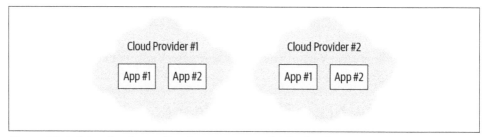

Figure 12-1. Joint cloud—applications run on multiple clouds

App #1 and App #2 can be run on either of the cloud providers. You can also load balance each application across both clouds simultaneously, if desired. If one cloud becomes unavailable, the other cloud can take over responsibility for running the application.

Each application must be designed to run on either cloud provider, and the application can use either available provider to satisfy a given request. If one provider is unavailable, the other provider can take over to process requests for the application.

One major advantage of this approach is application resiliency. If a cloud provider experiences an issue, the application workload can be rerouted to the other cloud provider easily and relatively quickly. This lets the application continue functioning even if one provider has a massive failure.

This architecture is often cited as a solution to single-vendor cloud lock-in because you can easily switch your load between multiple cloud providers. However, this architecture also has significant disadvantages. For example, each development and operations team supporting the application must have an understanding of the workings of multiple cloud providers. This knowledge and understanding does not come for free. Similarly, each application must be tested and maintained on multiple cloud providers.

Additionally, when applications are written to support multiple cloud providers, they cannot take advantage of deeper feature capabilities provided by one particular provider. The application must be written to use the least common capabilities inherent in all the cloud providers being utilized.

In most cases, the shortcomings of this approach outweigh the perceived improvements in resiliency.

Selective cloud applications

This is when your company maintains relationships with multiple cloud providers, but any given application runs entirely on a single provider, as shown in Figure 12-2.

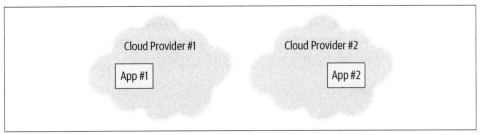

Figure 12-2. Selective cloud—each applications runs on a single selected cloud

You can see that each application is hosted on only a single cloud provider, but different applications may be hosted on different cloud providers.

In this scenario, a given component is designed to run and capable of running on only a single provider's cloud.

One perceived disadvantage of this approach is resiliency. If a cloud provider becomes unavailable, then the applications or services running on that provider will stop functioning. You cannot simply move traffic over to an alternate cloud provider. This is typically more of an intellectual issue than a practical one. It is rare for an entire cloud provider to become unavailable. Typically, only one or more availability zones or regions become unavailable. A properly written application can take advantage of multiple availability zones and regions to improve application resiliency without having to resort to using multiple cloud providers. Regions and availability zones for AWS are discussed in more detail in Chapter 15.

A real potential advantage of this architecture, though, is that individual applications or services can independently select which cloud provider they want to use based on whatever criteria makes sense for the application or service's owning team.

This architecture requires that each individual development and operations team supporting a given application learn and understand only how the single cloud provider it works with operates. Additionally, each team can take advantage of deeper feature capabilities unique to its specific cloud provider. The applications themselves can be designed, built, and optimized using cloud provider–specific best practices.

However, in this architecture the company must maintain multiple vendor relationships and agreements with each supported cloud provider. This is more of an administrative problem than a technical one, but it might be an issue for your organization.

In most cases, this approach gives you the desired flexibility of multiple clouds and the ability to do deep integrations with your cloud providers, without the application-level complexity that joint cloud applications require and without significantly sacrificing application resiliency.

Often organizations back into this particular architecture. One team or organization selects one cloud provider for its applications, while another team or organization selects another cloud provider for its own applications. The enterprise as a whole is multi-cloud, but individual applications are each single cloud.

Single cloud applications

This is the simplest design, in which a single cloud provider is used for all cloud needs within the company, as shown in Figure 12-3.

In this architecture, the company standardizes on a single cloud provider. It allows all development and operations teams to focus on the capabilities of that one provider. Knowledge can be easily shared across teams, and multiple teams can leverage a single set of best practices. And all applications can take advantage of the provider's full set of features.

Figure 12-3. Single cloud—applications all run on a single cloud provider

From a management perspective, having a single cloud provider simplifies vendor management. Additionally, since all traffic goes through a single provider, that provider has a higher volume usage, which may allow you to negotiate better pricing and other terms.

However, this solution obviously requires a strong commitment to a single cloud provider, which can be problematic for some companies. When a problem does occur, it is much harder to negotiate a solution when you are locked into a single vendor.

This solution may be the simplest to manage and control of all the options, but it limits the flexibility of your development teams.

Which Model? Which Cloud?

So which cloud model should you use? What makes sense for your company? The final answer depends on the needs of your company and your applications.

From an application perspective, the advantages of having an application runnable on multiple cloud providers is typically outweighed by the cost and complexity associated with maintaining multi-cloud-capable applications. Therefore, in almost all cases, the joint cloud applications model shown in Figure 12-1 does not make sense. If you are worried about maintaining high availability within your applications while tying them to a single vendor, consider using the high-availability solutions available from that vendor. For example, simply using multiple availability zones and multiple regions for your application running on AWS can dramatically improve your application's resiliency without incurring the costs and reduced capabilities of making your application run on multiple independent cloud providers.

When selecting a specific cloud provider, you should look at the following:

History of reliability
> How reliable has the service been historically? How quickly are outages dealt with? Do outages impact the entire provider, or do they impact only specific regions at any one time (allowing you to use multiple regions to improve resiliency)?

Capabilities of availability technologies
> Does the provider give you multiple availability zones and multiple independent geographic regions to allow fault isolation and failover? How independent are the zones and regions?

Availability of services
> Does the cloud provider have the types and depth of services you require?

Reason for moving to the cloud
> Why are you looking to move to the cloud? Is it to accelerate innovation or to help you in scaling? Whatever the reason, make sure it matches the cloud provider's capabilities.

If you choose to use multiple providers, do so because it makes sense for the given capabilities you require from those cloud providers. Don't do it to increase resiliency by using multiple providers. The reality is that the benefits are outweighed by the costs and disadvantages.

The Cloud in Summary

This chapter focused on how to use the cloud to architect scalable applications. We discussed how organizations mature in their ability to use and trust the cloud; common mistakes that organizations make when they adopt the cloud and the traps these mistakes can lead them into; and how and when to use multiple clouds in your applications.

CHAPTER 13

Five Industry Trends Changed by the Cloud

Cloud computing has changed the way we think about building and running our applications. But while how we build applications has changed around the cloud, the cloud itself has changed, and the way we think about the cloud has changed as well.

What Has Changed in the Cloud?

The cloud has matured over the past decade. Cloud providers have increased their product offerings. They no longer simply provide file storage and compute capacity. For example, AWS provides over 160 unique service offerings[1] to meet a variety of computing needs. Azure and Google offer hundreds more.

So what are the biggest changes the cloud is bringing to us and our applications? The following are five industry trends that have been driven, changed, and encouraged by the cloud.

Change #1: Acceptance of Microservice-Based Architectures

As we have discussed in this book, service- and microservice-based architectures have grown in popularity in recent years. Migrating applications to some form of a service-based architecture is becoming a standard technique in reducing technical debt and making applications easier to maintain.

As companies look toward moving their applications to the cloud, they are moving to the cloud usually as part of an overall product modernization strategy. This modernization strategy includes moving to a state-of-the-art application architecture. In recent years, this state-of-the-art application architecture involves using

---

[1] AWS had 165 services as of 2019.

microservices and other service-based architectures as part of that strategy. This is because technologies such as Docker have made microservice-based architectures a viable technology for application development.

Additionally, Function as a Service (FaaS) offerings, such as AWS Lambda, have given credibility to the creation of simple microservices without the need for servers. Advantages and disadvantages of this style of architecture decision aside, the creation of FaaS services in the cloud has also encouraged the creation of microservice-based architectures.

Realizing this push toward service- and microservice-based architectures, cloud providers have begun to provide higher-value managed offerings, such as the Elastic Container Service for use in managing service-based containers and AWS Lambda for running simple FaaS-based microservices.

Change #2: Smaller, More Specialized Cloud Services

As we modernize our applications and move them to the cloud, we begin looking at cloud services and how they can be utilized as extensions to our application's services. Capabilities historically provided within the applications are now provided by the cloud.

The major cloud providers now provide features such as databases, caching services, queuing services, logging services, content delivery network (CDN) capabilities, and transcoding services.

Change #3: Greater Focus on the Application

The cloud has shifted focus away from the creation and management of the infrastructure needed to run our applications, which lets us spend our time on more critical aspects of the application and the application environment.

Change #4: The Micro Startup

The cloud has made it possible for very small startups, often self-funded, single-person operations, to come into existence leveraging the inexpensive and scalable computing and other technology capabilities that the cloud offers.

It has never been easier for an individual with an idea to build that idea and potentially profit from it. The ability to build a compute ecosystem without the need to invest in an expensive infrastructure is helping new, fresh ideas come to market quickly. In particular, mobile applications such as online games have benefited greatly from this capability.

These startups quickly bring applications online to either flourish or fail, with minimal investment. For those that flourish, the cloud gives the applications the means to scale easily and inexpensively, letting companies invest in infrastructure at a rate proportional to their business needs. This has made it a lot easier to run and manage small startup companies financially.

Change #5: Security and Compliance Has Matured

In the early days of the cloud, security issues were often cited as one of the primary reasons why companies could not move their applications to the cloud.

Recognizing the need for improved security, cloud providers now provide better capabilities for securing cloud applications. Cloud companies also have added security assurances in the form of regulatory compliances such as PCI, SOC, and HIPPA.

Combined with a strong track record of visible high-quality security, these changes have removed security as an obstacle for a company looking at moving to the cloud.

Change Continues

Change is inevitable. The cloud has changed how we think about building and running our applications. We have begun building smaller, more specialized services. We have learned how to handle larger and larger quantities of data. We focus less on our applications' infrastructure and more on our applications. Smaller companies have become more viable, bringing fresh, new ideas and insights into the world. And security has become standard in everything we do.

The cloud has matured and caused our use and interactions with the cloud to mature. This will continue into the future, and we must constantly adapt to keep up with the changing landscape. Only then can our applications continue to grow and expand.

The remaining chapters in Part V will go into deeper detail on various aspects of cloud utilization and how they impact the development and architecture of your highly scaled applications.

CHAPTER 14

Types of SaaS and Tenancy

Software as a Service, or SaaS, is a term in common use today. At the most basic level, SaaS refers to software that is run and operated by a third party on its computers, rather than being run and operated by you on your own computers.

But SaaS can be a very misleading term. Some companies that have made on-premises (on-prem) software in the past have decided to "go into the cloud" and provide a SaaS offering. Often they do this by taking the same software they sell to customers and installing it on their own hardware in their own data center. They call this a "cloud" offering and call themselves a "SaaS" company.

Although this might be called a SaaS offering, it's nothing more than basic managed hosting. The company is hosting the software for you, but you still have your own instance of the software, and your company (or a third-party vendor) needs to manage that software instance. Such offerings have all the problems, version issues, and painful upgrades associated with on-prem software solutions. This results in slower new feature development, slower bug fixing, higher costs, and more downtime.

And they have all the same scaling problems of on-prem solutions.

They may call this SaaS, but you aren't really getting the benefits of SaaS.

Let's take a closer look at the different types of SaaS services to understand how they can be utilized to help you scale your applications.

Comparing Managed Hosting and Different Types of SaaS

There is a lot of confusion in the industry between managed hosting and SaaS. Further, there is confusion between different types of SaaS. To help clarify, I give these definitions:

Managed hosting

Managed hosting is when a vendor provides the hardware and provides assistance for the customer to run a specific instance of a software stack on that managed platform. The vendor may provide services that make the software installation and setup easier and reduce the complexity involved in managing the software. But managing the software is ultimately the responsibility of the customer. Capacity planning and scaling are the responsibility of the customer.

Multi-tenant SaaS

Multi-tenant SaaS is what we typically think of as "real" SaaS. This is where a vendor provides a software platform that will have many customers using the same running instance of the software platform. Customers are isolated from one another via the access controls in place within the software itself. Upgrades are usually done by the vendor transparently to customers.

Single-tenant SaaS

Single-tenant SaaS is when a vendor provides a software platform for its customers, but a given instance of the software (running on specific computers) is dedicated to a single customer. The vendor runs multiple stacks, typically one for each customer. Customers are isolated from one another via access to the entire software instance. Upgrades are usually done by the vendor transparently to customers.

Each of these three options has its own advantages and disadvantages.

Managed Hosting

Managed hosting is the most "bare-bones" option of the three I've outlined here. This is when a hosting provider gives you servers (virtual or physical) to run *your* software on *their* hardware. To increase its service's usefulness, the provider will often have packages in which it will automatically install common software packages onto its servers. This allows you to get up and running quickly and easily with a common software package without having to manage the installation of the software itself. A very common example of this is the WordPress blog content management system. Managed hosting providers will automatically install the WordPress software on the servers you have leased to get you started with building your blog or website.

However, these vendors typically do only what you, the customer, request of them. They typically do not automatically upgrade the software for you if new versions come out. Some may provide upgrade assistance, but usually only at your request and with your assistance. You typically have to worry about whether the version of software you are running has bugs or security holes in it, and deciding when and how to upgrade is your responsibility. You may not have to actually do the installation yourself, but you have many of the same worries around managing the software that you do with traditional on-prem software.

Managed hosting therefore typically requires a similar level of software management as on-prem software.

Multi-Tenant SaaS

Conceptually, multi-tenant SaaS is pretty simple. Multi-tenant SaaS vendors have many customers, potentially thousands, all running on a single instance of the application software. The customers share the same running software. The data of all the customers is typically on the same databases, but each customer's data is logically separated from other customers' data via business, software, and security rules and requirements.

There are many advantages of such an architecture. For the vendor:

- Upgrades can automatically be applied to all customers simultaneously. New features can be rolled out quickly and continuously.
- It's easy to reproduce customer problems "in house," because support has available the exact same environment that the customer is using.
- System resources, such as CPU, memory, and storage, are shared and divided among the customers as needed. This means that "spiky" usage by a single customer can be amortized out across the resources available to users that are not currently using their resources.
- The vendor can apply centralized brain-trust to the running of the software. This includes key operations functions such as security, availability, and scaling. By centralizing these functions, more expertise can be applied to a larger number of customers, and overall better solutions can be created.

As the number of customers increase, the economies of scale of managing all customers at once improves. It's much easier managing customers' instances in a centralized way than managing the complexity of individual customer instances and systems.

There are advantages for customers too:

- No need to worry about upgrading software, applying security patches, scaling hardware, storage, and networking...the vendor always manages this for you.
- New features that are rolled out are typically available to you more quickly and more easily than in traditional software.
- Critical bugs are typically fixed faster, and fixes are rolled out to production systems faster.
- More resources (both computer resources and brain-trust) can be applied to customers' needs, because resources can be more easily distributed and applied to a larger quantity of people.

Without a strong and reliable vendor providing the SaaS services, though, there can be disadvantages to this approach. Software can change suddenly and unexpectedly. If done at the wrong time for a given customer (such as at the end of a fiscal quarter, or during a busy shopping season), the results can be unnerving and problematic.

Overall, though, a multi-tenant SaaS platform run by a quality and responsible vendor provides significantly more advantages than disadvantages, and it is quickly becoming the norm for both consumer and enterprise customers in many businesses.

 Multi-tenant SaaS does not imply that all customers are on a single stack. A multi-tenant SaaS vendor may provide multiple stacks and have many customers on each of them. This is often done for geographic reasons (EU customers on a separate stack from US customers, for instance). But this can also be done for load balancing and scaling reasons.

Single-Tenant SaaS

Single-tenant SaaS is a lesser-known and lesser-used SaaS model, but it is still used in many important areas. Single-tenant SaaS is essentially a software vendor giving an entire instance of a software stack to a single customer. The vendor typically has multiple instances of its software stack running in order to manage multiple customers.

There are advantages to single-tenant SaaS:

- Customer data is usually more physically isolated from other customer data (note that this is a reasonable assumption but is not always the case).

- Since separate customers are using isolated sets of resources, customers don't "steal" resources from other customers.

- Each customer must have allocated sufficient resources for its own needs, and resources can't be shared across customers.

- It is possible for single customers to run a different version of software from other customers (the advantages/disadvantages of this could be the topic of an article in and of itself).

- Just like with multi-tenant SaaS, customers do not need to worry about upgrading software…the vendor always manages this for you.

Mixing Different Types of SaaS

Multi-tenant and single-tenant SaaS are not mutually exclusive. A single vendor may have a single application that has some customers running on a multi-tenant instance, while other customers (presumably the vendor's biggest or most critical customers) run on multiple single-tenant instances.

Typically, the difference between single-tenant SaaS and multi-tenant SaaS is transparent to the customer. While the customer may be aware and may have requested single-tenancy for contractual reasons with a vendor, the day-to-day experience of the customer usually is not impacted by this decision. In fact, some of the backend systems of a multi-tenant application may actually be single-tenant, and vice versa.

Common SaaS Characteristics

The key here, though, is that common characteristics apply to any true SaaS offering, whether single- or multi-tenant:

- They are software both provided *and* managed by a vendor.
- The customer does not need to worry about running and managing the software.
- Issues around software versioning are issues that the vendor deals with and the customer does not need to worry about.
- The customer can focus on just using the software…not on running the software.

These characteristics often do not apply to managed hosting.

SaaS Versus Managed Hosting

What's the biggest difference between SaaS and managed hosting? The biggest difference is ownership and decision making. In SaaS environments (single- or multi-tenant), decisions around upgrades and bug fix installation are owned by the service provider. In a managed hosting environment, decisions around upgrades and bug fix installation are owned by the customer. In true SaaS environments, customers do not have to worry about issues around software management. In managed hosting situations, they do.

Consider the hosting of a WordPress blog. Do you have your WordPress blog hosted on *wordpress.com*, or do you host it on a server at a company like GoDaddy? Or do you run the software on your own server (such as an EC2 instance)? All of these models exist, and all of them can in some ways be considered "cloud." None of these are on-prem. But not all of them are SaaS. *Wordpress.com* is an example of multi-tenant SaaS. The GoDaddy example could be a single-tenant SaaS or a managed hosting, depending on the capabilities they provide. The EC2 instance example is a true managed hosting example.

Summary

Each model has its advantages, as I've outlined in this chapter. Their suitability for a specific implementation will depend on the requirements and priorities in each individual case. For an enterprise that desires a high level of control over how the software is implemented and run—and has access to the necessary skill sets to manage it effectively—managed hosting can be a reasonable choice.

However, when people are shopping for a cloud or SaaS solution, they usually want the vendor to provide those skills and take care of issues like performance tuning, upgrades, and security. In such cases, it's crucial to beware of solutions that look like SaaS, and to make sure you understand your needs and how they map to the capabilities of your providers.

CHAPTER 15

Distributing Your Application in the AWS Cloud

We discussed in Chapter 2 the value of distributing an application across multiple data centers as a way of improving availability in a highly scaled environment.

The same philosophy applies in the cloud. As we put portions of our applications, or complete applications, into the cloud, we need to watch where in the cloud they are located. How distributed our applications are in the cloud is just as important as it is with normal data centers, particularly as applications scale. We also talked about the dangers of unknown common points of failure in shared infrastructure components, such as rack power supplies. The cloud, too, has common points of failure you should be aware of during your application deployment design process.

Due to the nature of how the cloud operates, the cloud makes understanding whether your application is properly distributed more challenging. The cloud also makes it more difficult to proactively make your application more distributed. Some cloud providers don't even expose enough information to let you know where, geographically, your application is running. This makes architecting to be resilient to infrastructure failure more difficult.

Luckily, AWS will help you distribute your application geographically. Although AWS won't tell you specifically where your application is running geographically, it will give you enough information to make proper scaling and availability decisions. However, there are subtleties to this information that you must understand in order to make proper decisions. Interpreting and understanding this information and using it to your advantage requires an understanding of how AWS is architected.

In this chapter, we will discuss the AWS architecture and how you can design and deploy your application to avoid common points of failure.

AWS Architecture

First, let's discuss some terms used within the AWS ecosystem.

AWS Region

An AWS region is a large area connection of cloud resources that represents a specific geographic area. In general, regions represent a portion of an individual continent or country (such as Western Europe, Northeastern Asia-Pacific, and United States East). They describe and document the geographic diversity of cloud resources. They are usually composed of multiple availability zones (AZs).[1]

An AWS region is identified by a string representing its geographical location. Table 15-1 gives the current list of AWS regions, their names, and what geographic regions they serve.

Table 15-1. AWS regions

Region name[a]	Geographic area covered
us-east-1	US East (N. Virginia)
us-east-2	US East (Ohio)
us-west-1	US West (N. California)
us-west-2	US West (Oregon)
ca-central-1	Canada (Central)
eu-west-1	EU (Ireland)
eu-west-2	EU (London)
eu-west-3	EU (Paris)
eu-central-1	EU (Frankfurt)
eu-north-1	EU (Stockholm)
ap-northeast-1	Asia Pacific (Tokyo)
ap-northeast-2	Asia Pacific (Seoul)
ap-northeast-3	Asia Pacific (Osaka)
ap-southeast-1	Asia Pacific (Singapore)
ap-southeast-2	Asia Pacific (Sydney)
ap-east-1	Asia Pacific (Hong Kong)
ap-south-1	Asia Pacific (Mumbai)
sa-east-1	South America (São Paulo)

[a] AWS regions and availability zones as of July 2019.

---

1 It is possible for a region to have only a single availability zone.

AWS Availability Zone

An AWS availability zone is a subset of an AWS region that represents cloud resources within a single region but is network topologically isolated from one another. AWS availability zones describe and document network topological diversity of cloud resources. If two cloud resources are in different availability zones, they can be assumed to be in distinct data centers, even if they are in the same AWS region. If two cloud resources are in the same availability zone, they can potentially both be in the same data center, floor, rack, or even physical server.

An AWS availability zone is identified by a string beginning with the name of the region the AZ is in, followed by a letter (a–z). For example, Table 15-2 shows some example availability zones and the regions they are in.

Table 15-2. AWS availability zone names (sampling)

Region name	AZ names
us-east-1	us-east-1a, us-east-1b, us-east-1c, us-east-1d, us-east-1e
us-west-1	us-west-1a, us-west-1b, us-west-1c
us-west-2	us-west-2a, us-west-2b, us-west-2c
ap-northeast-1	ap-northeast-1a, ap-northeast-1b, ap-northeast-1c
...	...

Data Center

This is not a term used within AWS vocabulary, but we will use it as we map typical noncloud terminology into AWS terminology.

A data center is a specific floor, building, or group of buildings constituting a single location of system resources, such as servers.

Our goal with our application is to distribute our application across multiple data centers. Hence, knowing how the data center terminology maps to actual cloud implementations is important.

Architecture Overview

Figure 15-1 shows at a high level what the AWS cloud architecture looks like. AWS is composed of several AWS regions, which are geographically distributed around the globe in order to provide high-quality access to most locations in the world. The AWS regions each have connections to the internet. The AWS regions themselves also are connected among themselves, but they use long-distance network connections similar to the rest of the internet.

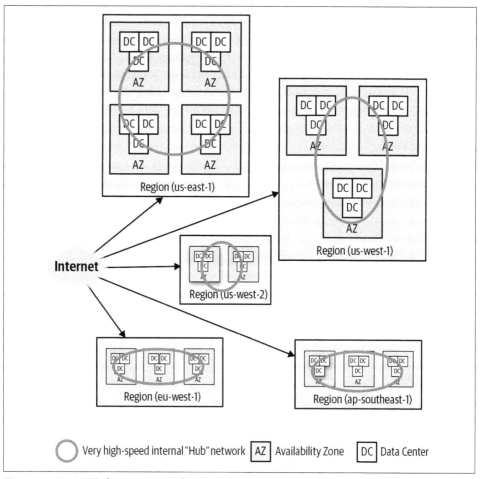

Figure 15-1. AWS data center architecture

A single AWS region is composed of one or more AWS availability zones. The AZs within a single region are connected via an extremely high-speed hub network link, as shown in Figure 15-2. The goal is to make access between any two servers within a region have similar performance characteristics without concern for the AZ in which the servers are located.

A given AZ is composed of one or more data centers, depending on the size of the AZ.

As you can see, the network topography is designed to make it easy to build an application within a single region but distributed across availability zones. This distribution is designed to give redundant systems failover opportunities in light of problems with individual data centers, while maintaining the ability for the independent components to communicate with one another at high speeds transparently, without regard to the availability zone they are in.

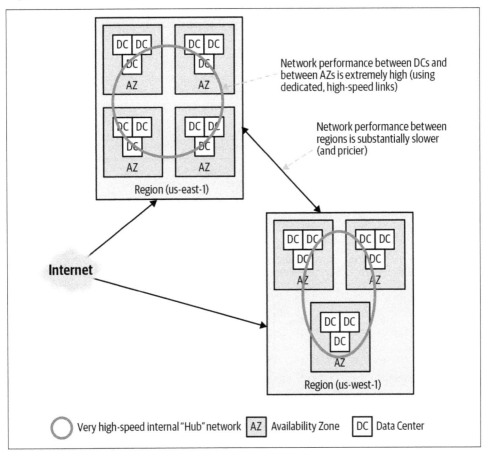

Figure 15-2. AWS region and availability zone network performance

 While you cannot pick what data centers your servers are located in, putting two servers in two availability zones can guarantee that the servers are in two data centers.

However, regions are designed so that an entire application would be contained within a single region and thus would not require high-speed communications with components contained in other regions. If an application wants to be in multiple regions, multiple copies of the application are typically run independently, one copy within each region desired. This makes it possible for individual geographic regions to have access to an instance of an application locally without suffering the cost of long-distance communication links. This is shown in Figure 15-3. This model is supported by the AWS network traffic costing model, which typically allows traffic between AZs within a single region is free, while traffic destined between regions or out from a region to the internet to be charged appropriately.

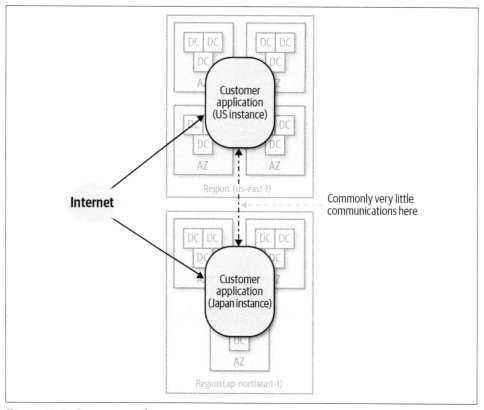

Figure 15-3. Customer architecture

This architecture is important not only from a cost standpoint but also from a latency standpoint (region-to-region network latency is higher than AZ-to-AZ). Additionally, this structure gives your application the ability to support various governmental regulations, such as the EU-US Privacy Shield[2] and the GDPR.[3]

---

2 The EU-US Privacy Shield, the successor to EU Safe Harbor, is a set of privacy principles that governs the transmission of data about EU citizens to locations outside of the EU. It often can matter where data is stored in order to comply with local laws, and AWS regions make it possible for applications to be built to support these laws and principles.

3 The GDPR, or General Data Protection Regulation, regulates how data about EU citizens must be handled.

Availability Zones Are Not Data Centers

Within a given account, an EC2 compute instance in one AZ (such as us-east-1a) and an EC2 instance in another AZ (such as us-east-1b) may safely be assumed to be in distinct data centers.

However, this is not necessarily true when you are using more than one AWS account. When you create an EC2 instance in account #1 that is in AZ us-east-1a, and an EC2 instance in account #2 that is in AZ us-east-1c, these two instances might, in fact, be in the same data center. They may actually be located on the same physical server!

Why is this the case? It is because the AZ names do not statically map directly to specific data centers. Instead, the data center(s) used for "us-east-1a" in one account might be different than the data center(s) used for "us-east-1a" in another account.

When you create an AWS account, they "randomly" create a mapping of availability zone names to specific data centers. This means that one account's view of "us-east-1a" will be physically present in a very different location than another account's view of "us-east-1a." This is demonstrated in Table 15-3. Here we show a selection of data centers (arbitrarily numbered 1 through 8) within a single region. Then we show a possible mapping between AZ names and those data centers for four sample accounts.

Table 15-3. Unexpected availability zone mappings

Data center	AWS account 1	AWS account 2	AWS account 3	AWS account 4	...
DC #1	us-east-1a	us-east-1d		us-east-1e	...
DC #2	us-east-1a	us-east-1c	us-east-1a	us-east-1a	...
DC #3	us-east-1b	us-east-1a	us-east-1d	us-east-1d	...
DC #4	us-east-1c		us-east-1a	us-east-1b	...
DC #5	us-east-1d	us-east-1b	us-east-1c	us-east-1c	...
DC #6	us-east-1e		us-east-1b		...
DC #7			us-east-1e		...
DC #8		us-east-1e			...

From this, you'll notice a few things. First, a single AZ for an account can, in fact, be contained in multiple distinct data centers. This means the two EC2 instances you create within a single account and a single AZ may be on the same physical server, or they could be in completely different data centers. Second, two EC2 instances created in different accounts may or may not be in the same data center, even if the AZs are different.

For example, in Table 15-3, if account #1 creates an instance in us-east-1b, and account #3 creates an instance in us-east-1d, those two instances will both be created in data center #3.

This is important to keep in mind for one simple reason: just because you have two EC2 instances in two accounts in two different AZs, that does not mean they can be assumed to be independent for availability purposes.

As discussed in Chapter 2, maintaining independence of replicated components is essential for availability and risk management purposes. However, when using multiple AWS accounts, the AWS AZ model does not enforce this. The AZ model can be used to enforce this only when dealing within a single AWS account.

Why would you ever want to use more than one AWS account? Actually, this is fairly common. Many companies create multiple AWS accounts used by different groups within the company. AWS might do this for billing purposes, permissions management, or other reasons. Sometimes security policies dictate the use of multiple AWS accounts.

When AWS announces an outage, it posts this outage on its service status website. But when it discusses where the outage has occurred, it will say that an outage impacts "some availability zones" in a given region but will not say which specific availability zones are impacted.

The reason for this is due to how the AWS availability zones are mapped: if AWS has a problem in, say, DC#4, that might mean your "us-east-1a" availability zone, whereas for the next person it might be their "us-east-1c" availability zone. AWS cannot give the name of a specific availability zone, because the name of the AZ is different for each account.

Why does AWS use this weird mapping? One of the main reasons is for load balancing. When people launch EC2 instances, they tend not to evenly distribute them across all availability zones. In fact, "us-east-1a" is a more common AZ for people to launch EC2 instances than "us-east-1e." This is governed as much by human nature as anything. If AWS did not do this artificial remapping, AZs earlier in the alphabet would be overloaded, whereas AZs later in the alphabet would be less loaded. By creating this artificial mapping, AWS is able to load balance usage more effectively.

Maintaining Location Diversity for Availability Reasons

How do you ensure that AWS resources you launch have redundant components that are guaranteed to be located in different data centers and therefore risk tolerant to outages?

There are a couple things you can do. First, make sure that you maintain redundant components in distinct AZs within a single account. If you have redundant components that are in multiple accounts, make sure you maintain redundancy in multiple AZs within each account individually. Don't compare AZs across accounts.

AWS—Mapping Availability Zones in Multiple Accounts

It is possible in AWS to determine whether or not two availability zones in two accounts are potentially in the same data center. Doing this requires use of the AWS Resource Access Manager and the AWS console.

Log in to the AWS console and click on the "Resource Access Manager" service.[4] On this page, look for the section titled "Your AZ ID" (at the time this was written, it was in the righthand column, about halfway down—see Figure 15-4).

What you will see is a mapping of AWS availability zone names (such as us-east-1a and us-east-1b) to what are called AZ IDs. You can think of an AZ ID as essentially the name of a specific physical data center.

The AZ IDs are numbers that are consistent for all AWS accounts. While you cannot compare AZ names (such as us-west-2a) across accounts, you can compare AZ IDs (such as usw2-az2) across accounts. Using the AZ ID, you can determine whether two availability zones in two different accounts are in the same data center.

This table provides the availability zone name to AZ ID mapping for a given account in a given AWS region. To check the AZ ID for a different account, log in to the console using that account. To check the AZ ID mapping for a different region, select the desired region from the region dropdown in the console's upper-right corner.

---

4 Or you can access the Resource Access Manager console (*http://console.aws.amazon.com/ram*) directly.

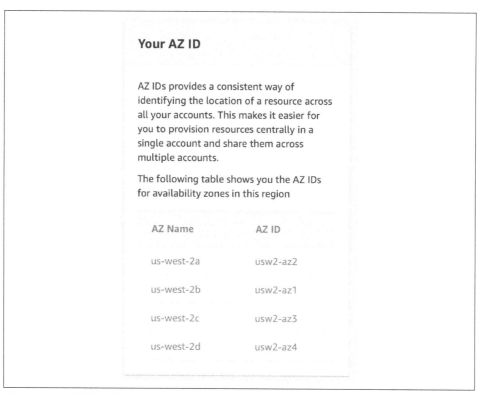

Your AZ ID

AZ IDs provides a consistent way of identifying the location of a resource across all your accounts. This makes it easier for you to provision resources centrally in a single account and share them across multiple accounts.

The following table shows you the AZ IDs for availability zones in this region

AZ Name	AZ ID
us-west-2a	usw2-az2
us-west-2b	usw2-az1
us-west-2c	usw2-az3
us-west-2d	usw2-az4

Figure 15-4. AWS AZ mapping to data center IDs for a given region in a given account

Distributing Your Application

As you decide which availability zones your application will use, you pick the availability zones based on removing common points of failure. Using AWS availability zones is a good start at making sure you can remove common failure points, but you must be careful and understand how AZ mapping really works, especially when you are using applications that span multiple AWS accounts. Without this understanding, you may have hidden common points of failure that can reduce your application's true availability.

CHAPTER 16

Managed Infrastructure

When you think of the cloud, what do you think of? If you are like most people, you think of the following:

- File storage (such as Amazon S3, Azure Cloud Storage, or Google Cloud Storage)
- Servers (such as Amazon's EC2, Azure Servers, or Google Compute Engine)

And in fact, you can utilize the cloud efficiently and effectively using only these two types of resources.

However, cloud companies offer a wide variety of managed services that you can take advantage of to ease your management load, increase your availability, and improve your scalability. Knowing how these components are organized and managed can help determine which capabilities you wish to utilize for your application.

While the concepts discussed here apply to all cloud providers, for this chapter we will focus on AWS for our examples and illustrations.

Structure of Cloud-Based Services

There are three basic types of cloud-based services:

- Raw resource
- Server-based managed resource
- Serverless managed resource

Figure 16-1 illustrates these three types. Raw resources provide basic server virtualization support and nothing else. The application and the operating system that runs the application on the virtualized hardware are all owned and managed by the consumer. Only the virtualization layer is managed by the cloud provider. Server-based managed resources follow the same basic system architecture; they still run software on a virtualized server. The difference is that the software that runs on the server is also managed by the cloud provider. In a serverless managed resource, the software running the resource is managed by the cloud provider, but the infrastructure running the software is invisible to the consumer, and the consumer is not impacted by how the infrastructure is managed.

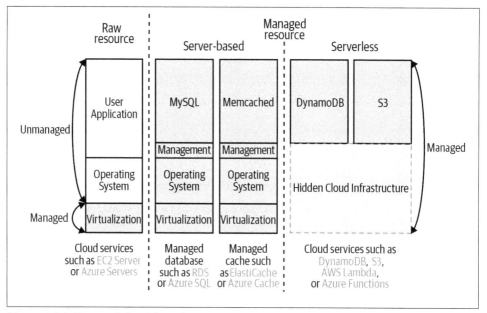

Figure 16-1. Types of cloud-based services

Let's look at each of these three types of cloud services in greater detail.

Raw Resource

A raw cloud resource provides basic capabilities to the user and provides only basic management. An example of a raw cloud resource is Amazon EC2 or Azure Virtual Server, each of which provides raw server capabilities in a managed manner.

The cloud provides management of the basic server virtualization layer and the creation of the instance and its initial filesystem. However, after the instance is up and running, the operation of the server itself is opaque to the cloud provider (see Figure 16-2).

The cloud provider manages the data flowing into and out of the instance (the network), as well as the CPU and the utilization of the CPU. But the provider does not know anything about what is running within the server itself, nor does it monitor anything that goes on in the server.

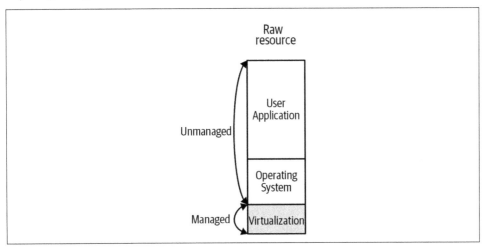

Figure 16-2. Raw resource management responsibility

For cloud providers like AWS, this is intentional. What runs on the server is your business, and AWS does not want to be responsible for any aspect of the software running on it. AWS's line of responsibility ends at the entry/exit points to the virtual server itself. AWS even has a name for this: it's called the AWS Shared Responsibility Model. For each of AWS's services, this model describes what is the responsibility of AWS and what is the responsibility of the customer. In the case of EC2, the Shared Responsibility Model describes the end of AWS's responsibility at the virtualization layer, and the start of the customer's responsibility at the operating system layer.

Where you can see the impact of using raw resources

You can see the impact of this in a couple different ways.[1] For EC2 instances, look at the metrics that AWS collects and provides to you via CloudWatch. All of the metrics are network-level metrics, such as:

- The amount of network traffic to/from the instance
- How much data is read/written to the disks
- The amount of CPU that is being consumed

But missing from this list are some obviously useful metrics that it does not track:

---

1 More information on what AWS monitors with CloudWatch is available at *https://oreil.ly/qKvOk*.

- Amount of free memory and disk space
- Number of processes running
- Swap or paging activity
- Which processes are consuming the most resources

These metrics don't exist because they depend on the operating system used on the instance, which is not managed by the cloud provider.

You can also see the impact of this in the access control to the instance. AWS manages network-level access to your instance (via ACLs), but you are responsible for user login capabilities to the instance (operating system).

Server-Based Managed Resource

A server-based managed resource is a resource that provides a full stack managed solution for a specific cloud capability. An example of a server-based managed resource is Amazon RDS database or Microsoft Azure SQL database. These services provide a managed database application running on top of a managed server infrastructure. Figure 16-3 shows how server-based managed resources are managed.

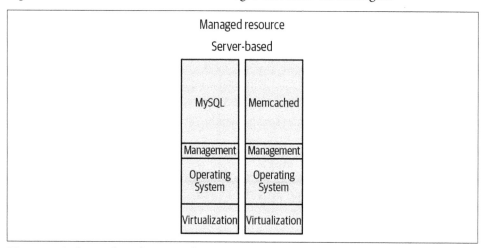

Figure 16-3. Server-based managed resource management responsibility

A managed database solution such as Amazon Relational Database Service (RDS) or Microsoft's Azure SQL runs the database and special management software on an existing managed server, making it possible for the entire stack, server, and software on the server to be managed by the cloud provider. The database software is an industry-standard database (such as MySQL, PostgreSQL, or SQL Server) running in a completely managed manner on top of a standard managed server. These services provide a complete managed database solution, top to bottom.

Take a look at Figure 16-1 again, and you can see how RDS is structured. (Figure 16-3 shows a close-up view of this managed stack.) Basically, when you launch an RDS instance, you launch an EC2 instance that is running a specific OS, special management software, and the database software itself. Amazon manages not only the EC2 server but the entire software stack as well, including the OS and database software.

Where you can see the impact of using server-based managed resources

You can see the impact of this by looking at the CloudWatch metrics provided by RDS instances. Besides the basic EC2 instance information, you get additional monitoring about the database itself, such as the following:

- Number of connections made to the database
- Amount of filesystem space the database is consuming
- Number of queries being run on the database
- Replication delay

These metrics are available only from the OS and the database software itself.

Another way to understand the impact is to consider the type of configuration you can perform. No longer is the configuration just basic information about the server (network connections and disks connected)—you can also configure information about the database itself, such as maximum number of connections, caching information, and other configuration and tuning parameters.

Serverless Managed Resource

Serverless managed resources are resources that provide a specific capability, but do not expose the server infrastructure the capability is running on. There are several examples of this in AWS, including Amazon S3, DynamoDB, and AWS Lambda. From Microsoft, Azure Functions is an example of such a serverless managed service. Figure 16-4 shows how serverless managed resources are architected and managed.

Let's take a look at a great example of a serverless managed storage service, Amazon S3. This service provides cloud-based file storage and transmission. When you store a file in S3, you communicate directly with the S3 service. There is no *server* or *servers* that are allocated on your behalf to perform the actions. The fact that there might be one or more servers running behind the scenes to perform the request is invisible to you.

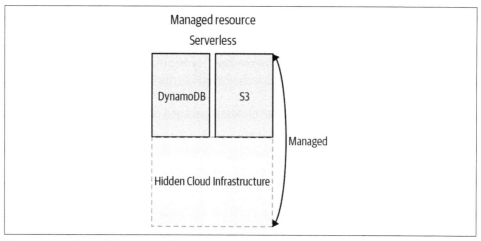

Figure 16-4. Serverless managed resource management responsibility

The entire operation is managed, but you only have visibility into, and the ability to control, the exposed software interface provided by the service (in the case of S3, that is uploading files, downloading files, deleting files, and so on). You have no visibility into, nor the ability to control, the underlying operating system or the servers that service is running on. These servers are shared among all users of the service, and as such they are managed and controlled by Amazon without your involvement.

Another great example of a serverless service is AWS Lambda. This service provides cloud-based function execution. As is the case in Amazon S3, there is no *server* or *servers* that are allocated on your behalf to perform the actions. The fact that there might be one or more servers running behind the scenes to perform the request is invisible to you.

Why serverless?

One of the great advantages of serverless services, such as these is their ability to scale without the need for you to take additional actions to allocate resources. If traffic to your application increases suddenly, Amazon will automatically apply the appropriate resources to handle your increase in Amazon S3 or AWS Lambda needs. You do not need to allocate additional resources for this to happen; it is all managed by AWS.

This is opposed to server-based managed services, which require you to take actions based on expected traffic load. When you create an Amazon RDS database instance, you have to size it to match your expected traffic needs. If your traffic needs fall below this level, you waste resources. If your traffic needs fall above this level, you risk running out of database capacity and starving your requests. You have to manage the allocation of resources applied to your application.

Implications of Using Managed Versus Non-Managed Resources

When a service or a part of a service is managed, there are many advantages for you, the user of the service. Here are some in particular:

- You do not need to install or update the software of a managed system.
- You do not need to tune or optimize the system (but you may have some capabilities to do so via the cloud provider).
- You do not need to monitor and validate that the software is performing as expected.
- The cloud provider can provide monitoring data for you to consume, if you desire, without additional software or capabilities.
- The cloud provider can provide backup and replication capabilities for the service.
- The cloud provider can provide a higher level of security to your service.

There are also disadvantages to managed components:

- You typically do not have the ability to significantly change how the software performs its operations.
- You do not have the ability to control when and how the software is upgraded or the version of software that is running.[2]
- You are limited to the capabilities offered by the cloud provider for monitoring and configuring the service.

When a service or a part of a service is nonmanaged, there are some advantages for you, the user of the service. Here are some in particular:

- You can control what software is running on the service, what version is running, and how it is set up.
- You control when and how upgrades are performed, or if they are performed.
- You can monitor and control the software in whatever manner you want, using whatever mechanisms you want.

There are also disadvantages to nonmanaged components:

---

2 However, the cloud provider can provide you some of these capabilities; for example, RDS provides a range of database versions that it supports, but not all versions are available. In managed systems like S3, you have no control over the software upgrade process at all.

- Nothing is free. You are completely responsible for all management and maintenance that the system requires.

- You must make sure you perform your own backup and data replication.

- You must monitor your software to ensure that it is functioning correctly—if you do not, no one will let you know when it fails.

- If the software breaks or fails, you alone are responsible for fixing it. The cloud provider cannot help.

- You have to manage the security of the service—your cloud provider can't help you nearly as much.

Summary

Understanding whether a service is managed or not, and whether it is server-based or serverless, can help you make the best use of the service and help you make decisions on how to utilize the service, especially in a highly scaled application.

CHAPTER 17

Cloud Resource Allocation

As you build a highly scaled application, one important step for deploying the application is allocating the resources necessary to operate the application. Resources can be anything from computer instances to data storage. How you allocate those resources, and how you determine what the allocation should be, matters to your application. If you allocate too few resources to an application, you can starve the application and create an availability problem. If you allocate too many resources, you can waste money by having too many resources lying around idle and unused.

This is the struggle with all highly scaled applications, and it is especially a problem for highly spiky application usage. If your application has relatively short periods of time with extremely high usage, and significantly lower usage at other times, deciding how to allocate resources efficiently can be a problem.

This is one of the key advantages of the cloud. With the cloud, you can dynamically allocate resources on an as-needed basis in order to handle these spiky needs efficiently, without leaving a significant amount of unused resources lying around during nonbusy times.

But managing cloud resources is not a simple task and takes care and consideration. Successfully managing your cloud resource allocation needs without creating waste or starvation requires knowledge of how resource allocation works in the cloud. You must understand how cloud resources are allocated, consumed, and, most importantly, charged.

Cloud resources can be divided reasonably into two categories:

- Usage-based resources
- Allocated-capacity resources

All cloud resources fall into one of these two general categories, and the process you use to manage those resources varies considerably depending on which category a resource falls into.

Let's talk about each of these two types of resource usage categories.

Usage-Based Resources Allocation

Usage-based resources are cloud resources that are not allocated but are consumed at whatever rate your application requires. You are charged only for the amount of the resource you consume. There is no allocation that is required for the resource.

You can recognize usage-based cloud resources by the following characteristics:

- There is no allocation step involved, and hence no capacity planning is required.
- If your application needs fewer resources, you use fewer resources and your cost is lower.
- If your application needs more resources, you use more resources and your cost is higher.
- Within reason, you can scale from a very tiny amount consumed to a huge amount consumed without taking any steps to scale your application or the cloud resource it is consuming.
- The phrase "within reason" is defined entirely by the cloud provider and its abilities.
- You typically have no visibility into how the resources are allocated or scaled. It is all invisible to you.

A classic example of usage-based cloud resources is Amazon S3. With S3, you are charged for the amount of data you are storing and the amount of data you transfer. You do not need to determine ahead of time how much data storage you require or how much transfer capacity you require. Whatever amount you require (within system limits) is available to you whenever you require it, and you pay only for the amount you use.

Here are additional examples of usage-based resources:

- Azure Cloud Storage
- AWS Lambda
- Azure Functions
- Amazon Simple Email Service

These services are easy to manage and scale because no capacity planning is required. This seemingly "magic" materialization of the resources necessary for your application using a usage-based resource is one of the true benefits of the cloud. It is made possible by the multi-tenant nature of these cloud services.

Behind a service like Amazon S3 is a huge amount of disk storage and a huge number of servers. These resources are allocated as needed to individual requests from individual users. If your application has a spike in the number of requests it requires, the necessary resources are automatically allocated from a shared availability pool.

This availability pool is shared by all customers, and so it is a potentially huge pool of resources. As your application's resource spike ebbs, another user's application might begin to spike, and those resources are then allocated to that user's application. This is done completely transparently.

As long as the pool of available capacity is large enough to handle all the requests and all the resource usage spikes occurring across all users, there is no starvation by any consumer. The larger the scale of the service (the more users that are using the service), the greater the ability of the cloud provider to average out the usage spikes and plan enough capacity for all the users' needs.

Large Consumers

This model works as long as no single user consumes a significant portion of the total resources available from the cloud provider. If a single customer is large enough to represent a significant portion of the resources made available for the service by the cloud provider, that customer can experience resource starvation during peak usage and potentially affect the capacity available to other customers as well.

For services like Amazon S3, the scale of the service is so massive that no single customer represents a significant portion of usage, and the resource allocation of S3 remains magical.[1]

However, even Amazon S3 has its limits. If you run an application that uses significant quantities of data transferred or stored, you can run into some of the limits S3 imposes in order to keep other users from experiencing resource starvation. As such, a large consumer of S3 resources can reach these artificial limits and experience resource starvation itself. This typically happens only if you are talking about data storage and transfer in the petabyte range.

---

[1] According to the most recent published Amazon data I could find, in 2013 S3 stored two trillion objects. That's five objects for every star in the Milky Way. (See "Amazon S3–Two Trillion Objects, 1.1 Million Requests/Second" (https://oreil.ly/xUHuy).)

Even if you do consume S3 resources at these huge levels, there are ways you can move your usage around to reduce the impact of the limits. Additionally, you can contact Amazon and request that these limits be increased. They will increase those limits in specific areas as you require, and these limit increases are then fed into Amazon's capacity planning process so they can ensure that there are sufficient resources available to meet your needs and everyone else's.

Allocated-Capacity Resource Allocation

Allocated-capacity resources are cloud resources that are allocated in discrete units. You specify how much of a specific type of resource you need, and you are given that amount. This amount is allocated to your use, and you are allocated that amount independent of what your real needs are at the moment.

Allocated-capacity cloud resources can be recognized by the following characteristics:

- They are allocated in discrete units.
- You specify how many units you want, and they are allocated for your use.
- If your application uses less of the resource, the allocated resources remain idle and unused.
- If your application needs more of the resource, the application becomes resource starved.
- Proper capacity planning is important to avoid both over- and underallocation.

The classic example of allocated-capacity cloud resources is servers, such as Amazon EC2 instances. You specify how many instances you want as well as the size of the servers, and the cloud allocates them for your use. Additionally, managed infrastructure components such as cloud databases often use an allocated capacity model. In each of these cases, you specify the number of units and their size, and the cloud provider allocates the units for your use.

Here are additional examples of allocated-capacity resources:

- Amazon RDS
- Amazon Aurora
- Azure SQL
- Amazon ElastiCache
- Amazon Elasticsearch Service
- Azure Cache

But there are other examples of allocated-capacity cloud resources that operate a bit differently—for example, Amazon DynamoDB. Using this service, you can specify how much capacity you want available for your DynamoDB tables.[2] Capacity is not measured in units of servers but in units of *throughput capacity units*. You allocate how much capacity you want to provide to your tables, and that much capacity is available for your use to that table. If you don't use that much capacity, the capacity goes unused. If your application uses more than the capacity you have allocated, your application will be resource starved until you allocate more capacity. As such, these *capacity units* are allocated and consumed in a manner very similar to *servers*, even though on the surface they look very different. Table 17-1 shows several major AWS allocated-capacity resource services and the units of allocation utilized by each service.

Table 17-1. Allocated-capacity resource services' units of allocation

AWS service	Capacity allocation unit	Allocation attributes
Amazon EC2	Instance-Hours	Instance size Hours operating
Amazon RDS	Instance-Hours	Database size Hours operating
Amazon Aurora	Instance-Hours	Database size Hours operating
Amazon ElastiCache	Instance-Hours	Cache size Hours operating
Amazon DynamoDB (Allocated)	Throughput Capacity Units	Allocated writes Allocated reads
Amazon DynamoDB (On-demand)	Request Units	Utilized writes Utilized reads
Amazon DynamoDB (Data storage)[a]	GB Stored	On-demand storage consumed

[a] Data storage for DynamoDB is a usage-based resource. It's included in this table to illustrate that a service may use multiple types of allocation mechanisms simultaneously.

Changing Allocations

Typically, capacity is allocated in discrete steps (a server costs a certain amount per hour; DynamoDB capacity units cost a certain amount per hour). You can change the number of servers allocated to your application or the number of capacity units allocated to your DynamoDB table, but only in discrete steps (the size of your server or the size of a capacity unit). Although there can be steps of various sizes available (such as different server sizes), you must allocate a whole number of units at a time.

---

2 DynamoDB also supports an on-demand pricing model, which behaves more like a usage-based resource.

It is your responsibility to ensure that you have enough capacity at hand. This might involve performing capacity planning exercises similar to those that you perform for traditional data center–based servers. You may very well allocate capacity based on expected demand and leave the number alone until you perform a review and determine that your capacity requirements have changed. This is typical of non-cloud-based server allocation but can also be used in cloud-based server allocation. However, there are other, more automated methods for changing allocation capacity.

Automated Allocation of Resource Capacity

Cloud allocation changes are easier to perform than traditional capacity changes in a data center. As such, algorithms can be used to perform your allocation automatically. For example:

On demand
> You can use a static allocation and then wait until you have consumed most of your allocated capacity. At that point, you can increase your capacity allocation as needed.

Fixed schedule
> You can automatically change your allocation based on a fixed schedule that matches your usage patterns. For instance, you could increase the number of servers available during heavily used daylight hours and decrease the number of servers during lesser-used nighttime hours.

Automatic (autoscaled)
> You can monitor specific metrics of your resources and determine when they are heavily utilized and when they are lightly utilized. Then, based on this data, you can dynamically and automatically allocate additional resources or remove excessive resources as needed. You could build this auto scale into your application or make use of cloud-provided auto scale mechanisms, such as Amazon EC2 Auto Scaling, which automatically allocates and frees EC2 instances based on configured metrics and criteria.

Whichever mechanism you choose to determine and change capacity, it is important to note that whatever capacity you currently have allocated is all that is available to you, and you could still end up with capacity allocated (and charged) to you that is not being used. Even worse, you could find yourself resource starved because you do not have enough capacity.

Issues with Automatic Allocation

Even if you use an automated allocation scheme such as Amazon EC2 Auto Scaling to give your application additional capacity when it is needed, that does not mean that the algorithm auto scaling uses to change your capacity can notice the need fast enough before your application becomes resource starved. This is especially problematic when your resource needs are extremely spiky in nature. This phenomenon is called *capacity allocation skew*, and it can lead to resource starvation or idle wasted resources, even when using an automatically scaled (auto scaled) allocation method.

As an example, consider Amazon's Elastic Load Balancer (ELB). This is a service that provides a load balancer to your application that automatically scales in size to handle whatever quantity of traffic has been sent to it. If you are receiving very little traffic, ELB will change the servers it is using for your load balancer to be smaller and fewer in number. If you are receiving a lot of traffic, ELB will automatically change the servers used for your load balancer to larger servers and put more of them into service. All of this is automatic and transparent to you as the application owner. This is how ELB is able to provide a load balancer at a very low entry price point, yet let the same load balancer scale to handle huge quantities of traffic (with a corresponding price increase), and all automatically. This saves you money when your traffic is light yet scales to your higher traffic needs when necessary.

However, there are places where the specifics of how this ELB automated allocation mechanism becomes visible in a negative way. If you receive a sudden spike in traffic, say, because your site suddenly goes viral due to a social media campaign, your load balancer might not be able to resize itself fast enough. The result? For a period of time after the traffic increase starts, your load balancer might be resource starved, causing page requests to be slow or to fail, creating a poor user experience. This situation will automatically correct as ELB determines your increased capacity needs and scales your load balancer up to larger servers and more of them. This scaling, though, can take a few minutes to complete. In the meantime, your users are having a poor experience, and availability suffers.

To combat this effect, Amazon lets you contact representatives and warn them of a coming change in traffic use patterns, allowing them to *prewarm* your load balancer.[3] This process of prewarming effectively scales your load balancer to use larger servers (and more of them) early, before the traffic spike occurs. This prewarming process, however, works only if you know you will experience a sudden rise in traffic. It doesn't help at all if the traffic spike is sudden or unexpected.

---

3 For more information, see "Best Practices in Evaluating Elastic Load Balancing" (*https://oreil.ly/SY8uc*) in the AWS ELB documentation.

Dynamic Allocation, Dynamic Cost

You typically can change your allocated capacity as often as you want,[4] increasing and decreasing it as your needs require.

This is one of the advantages of the cloud. If you need five hundred servers one hour and only two hundred the next hour, you are charged for five hundred servers for one hour and only for two hundred servers for the next hour. It's clean and simple.

However, because of this essentially infinite flexibility in the amount of capacity you can allocate, you typically pay a premium price for these resources. Flexibility costs money.

But what if your needs are more stable? What if you will *always* need at least two hundred servers allocated? Why pay for the ability to be flexible in the number of servers you need on an hour-by-hour basis when your needs are much more stable and fixed?

Reserved capacity

This is where *reserved capacity* comes into play. Reserved capacity is the ability for you to commit to your cloud provider up front that you will consume a certain quantity of resources for a period of time (such as one to three years). In exchange, you receive a favorable rate for those resources.

Reserved capacity does not limit your flexibility in allocating resources; it only guarantees to your cloud provider that you will consume a certain quantity of resources.

Suppose, for example, that you have an application that requires two hundred servers continuously, but sometimes your traffic spikes so that you need to have up to five hundred servers allocated at times. You can use auto scaling to automatically adjust the number of servers dynamically. Your usage in servers, therefore, varies from a minimum of two hundred servers to a maximum of five hundred servers.

Because you will always be using at least two hundred servers, you can purchase two hundred servers' worth of reserved capacity. Let's say you purchase two hundred servers for one full year. You will pay a lower rate for those two hundred servers, but you will be paying for those servers all the time. That's fine, because you are using them all the time.

For the additional three hundred servers, you can pay the normal (higher) hourly rate, and you pay only for the time you are using those servers.

---

4 There are sometimes restrictions, such as on DynamoDB, for which there are limitations to how often you can change capacity.

Reserved capacity provides a way for you to receive capacity at a lower cost in exchange for committed allocation of those resources.[5]

Pros and Cons of Usage-Based Versus Allocated-Capacity

As outlined in Table 17-2, usage-based resource allocation methods and allocated-capacity resource allocation methods have some advantages and disadvantages.

Table 17-2. Cloud resource allocation comparison

	Allocated-capacity	Usage-based
Service examples (Amazon AWS)	EC2, ELB, RDS, DynamoDB, Azure SQL, Azure Servers	S3, Lambda, SES, SQS, SNS, Azure Functions
Requires capacity planning	Yes	No
Charges based on	Capacity allocated	Capacity consumed
What happens when underutilized	Capacity is idle (wasted)	N/A
What happens when overutilized	Application is starved (not enough capacity, potential availability outage)	N/A
Can capacity be reserved to save money?	Yes	No
How can capacity be scaled?	Manual or automated allocation change controlled by you	N/A
How are usage spikes handled?	Potential usage starvation during spike or capacity ramp-up	Automatic and transparent
What happens with excess capacity?	Excess capacity goes unused	Used by other customers

The allocated-capacity method requires forward-based capacity planning, while the usage-based method does not. With allocated-capacity resource allocation, you are charged based on how much capacity you have requested rather than on how much you are actually consuming. This means that you may end up with wasted capacity, or you can resource-starve your application.

---

5 Using reserved capacity also guarantees that the specific type of instance will be available in your specific desired availability zone, when you want it. Without having reserved capacity, it is possible that you could request a specific type of instance in a specific availability zone, and AWS would not be able to honor the request.

CHAPTER 18

Serverless and Functions as a Service

Function as a Service (FaaS) offerings, such as AWS Lambda and Azure Functions, are relatively new software execution environments that have given credibility to the creation of simple microservices without the need for servers. The industry has coined the term *serverless* to refer to these types of execution environments.[1]

FaaS offerings provide event-driven compute capabilities without the need to purchase, set up, configure, or maintain servers. FaaS offerings such as AWS Lambda and Azure Functions give you virtually unlimited scalability with the ability to pay at a subsecond-metered level.

Services such as AWS Lambda can scale to almost any rational scaling size necessary, without any actions required to make that happen. This is the true power of FaaS.

Here are some typical use cases for FaaS:

- Image transformation for newly uploaded images
- Real-time metric data processing
- Streaming data validation, filtering, and transformation

It is best suited for any sort of processing where:

- Operations need to be performed as the result of an event occurring in your application or environment
- A data stream needs filtering or transformation

---

1 The term *serverless* also applies to cloud service offerings, such as DynamoDb, S3, and Azure Cloud Storage. This is a different interpretation of the term than what applies to Functions as a Service (FaaS).

- Edge validation or regulation of inbound data is necessary

There currently is a lot of hype around FaaS. However, FaaS services aren't for everything. Their real power is useful in specific types of architectures. The following are some specific types of applications that can effectively make use of FaaS. These examples make use of the AWS cloud and AWS Lambda FaaS service.

Example Application #1: Event Processing

Consider a photograph management application. Users can upload photos to the cloud, which are then stored in a storage service such as S3. The application displays thumbnail versions of those pictures and lets users update attributes associated with those pictures, such as name, location, names of people in the picture, and so on.

This simple application can utilize AWS Lambda to process images after they are uploaded to S3. When a new picture is uploaded, a Lambda function can be automatically triggered that takes the picture and creates a thumbnail version of that picture and stores the thumbnail version in S3. Additionally, a different Lambda function can take various characteristics of the picture (such as size, resolution, etc.) and store that metadata in a database. The picture management application can then provide capabilities for manipulating the metadata in the database.

This architecture is shown in Figure 18-1.

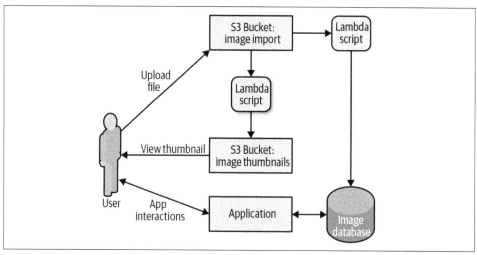

Figure 18-1. File upload Lambda usage

The picture management application does not need to be involved in the file upload process at all. It can rely on standard S3 upload capabilities and the two Lambda functions to do all processing necessary to complete the file upload process. So the picture management application has to deal only with what it is good at: manipulating metadata in the database for existing pictures.

Example Application #2: Mobile Backend

Consider a mobile game that stores user progress, trophies, and high scores in the cloud, making that data available for a shared community as well as enabling device portability for individual users.

This application involves a series of APIs on the backend that are created so that the mobile application can store data in the cloud, retrieve user information from the cloud, and then perform community interactions. The cloud backend runs on AWS.

The necessary APIs are created by using an API Gateway[2] that connects with a series of Lambda functions. The Lambda scripts perform the operations necessary, in conjunction with some form of database, to handle the cloud backend for the mobile game.

This architecture is shown in Figure 18-2.

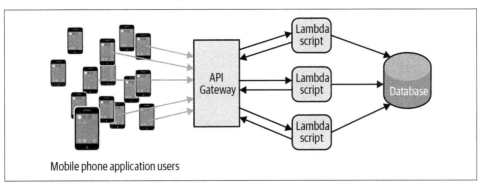

Figure 18-2. Mobile backend Lambda usage

In this model, no servers are needed on the backend, and all scaling is handled automatically.

Example Application #3: Internet of Things Data Intake

Consider an application that takes data from a huge quantity of data sensors deployed around the world. Data from these sensors arrives regularly. On the server side, this results in an enormous quantity of data being regularly presented to the application for storage in some form of data store. The data is used by some backend application,

---

2 The Amazon API Gateway is an API creation service that is designed to work closely with AWS Lambda.

which we will ignore for this example. All we will be concerned with is the data intake process.

The data intake needs to validate the data, perhaps perform some limited processing on the data, and store the resulting data in the data store.

This is a simple application that performs only basic data validation and verification and stores the data in a backend data store for future processing. However, though the application is simple, it must run at a massive scale, potentially in the order of millions or billions of data intake events per minute. The exact scale is dependent on the number of sensors and the amount of data each sensor generates.

This architecture makes use of a data intake pipeline[3] that sends data to an AWS Lambda function that performs any necessary filtering or processing of the data before it's stored in the data store.

This architecture is shown in Figure 18-3.

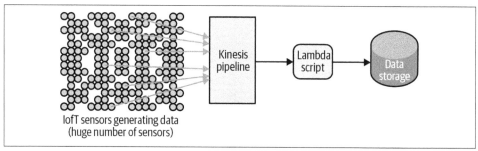

Figure 18-3. Internet of Things sensor intake example

Lambda is well suited to handling the huge volume of data that must be ingested at a high speed regularly.

Advantages and Disadvantages of FaaS

FaaS offerings have one primary advantage: scale. AWS Lambda, for example, is very good at handling massive scale loads without the need to increase the amount of infrastructure allocated to your application.

It accomplishes this by optimizing its operation for code that is relatively simple in nature, allowing it to be easily spun up on multiple servers in multiple stacks quickly and effectively, on an as-needed basis.

---

3 Amazon Kinesis is a real-time streaming data intake pipeline that is designed to handle the intake of vast data streams and works closely with AWS Lambda.

This is the sweet spot for FaaS: a small code footprint executed at mammoth scale. That sweet spot makes AWS Lambda an effective solution for all three of the example architectures we looked at.

So where should you not use FaaS? To answer that, let's look at the disadvantages of FaaS services:

- Implicit coding requirements (assumed simple, event-driven, fast-processing, limited operating environments)
- Typically complex configuration and setup
- Typically no native built-in staging or testing environments
- Typically no native deploy/rollback capabilities built in
- No or limited native development environment for building and testing FaaS functions

In short, FaaS is great for running small scripts at large scale, but it is poor at all of the other things necessary for a large-scale application deployment. It's ill equipped to perform complex calculations and complex interactions and is not a good fit for complex code and execution environments. The more complex the code, the less ideal it is for use in FaaS. There are companies focused on serverless computing that are working on solving some of these issues, such as improving the development and deployment environments. But these are new and untested tools and capabilities.

Used effectively, FaaS is a technology that will significantly help in your extreme scaling needs. However, be careful to limit its use to only those tasks for which it is well suited. For compute execution needs outside of the FaaS sweet spot, use other deployment/execution options.

Serverless Hype and the Future of FaaS

There are some people who believe that AWS Lambda and other FaaS offerings are "taking over the world" and will eventually cause traditional server-based computation and container technology (such as Docker and Kubernetes) to become obsolete. I firmly disagree with this assessment. FaaS computation services such as AWS Lambda and Azure Functions give a powerful, high-scale computation *option* for a specific class of computing needs. However, they will not "take over the world" or replace the need for and value of traditional server-based and container-based computation.

Be careful trying to force fit serverless functions into solving all your computing needs. There are people who are trying to make their applications run "100% on Lambda." FaaS computation is not a perfect solution for all computation needs, and it should not be force fit into that role. Container- and server-based software, in my opinion, will always represent a larger piece of the computation pie than serverless/ FaaS will.

Use the right tool for the right purpose and don't force fit FaaS into situations where it doesn't naturally fit.

CHAPTER 19

Edge Computing

What, exactly, is the edge? The edge is monitoring weather and drought conditions on a farm to ensure optimal crop production. The edge is an automated drone, flying solo, taking photographs or gathering environmental or geographical data. The edge is a semitruck transmitting information about where it is, its load, and its operating condition to a central transportation system. The edge is a smart home appliance that automatically knows when you are running low on something and assists you with ordering more. The edge is a smart home that monitors and keeps us safe, such as by shutting off a stove when a fire is detected or turning on an alarm when it knows you are no longer at home.

All of these are examples of edge computing. Each is an example of a novel use in and of itself. When we think about edge computing, these are the sorts of examples that come to mind. But what exactly is edge computing? Edge computing is taking part of your application and moving it closer to where the action is.

What do we mean by "the action"? By "the action," we mean the source of interesting data that you want to process. This might be the end user of the application or the system being controlled. Or it might be the thing at the end of your application that represents the reason your application exists…the thing it was designed and built for.

Edge computing is about putting computation close to the need for that computation. Edge computing is, quite simply, putting computation where it belongs.

So when we are monitoring drought conditions on a farm, we are gathering tons of data from far-reaching locations. And when we are talking about an automated drone, we are talking about keeping it in the air and free from the impact of wind and weather, without human involvement. And when we are talking about a semitruck, it's about gathering useful information such as where the truck is located, whether it is moving at a safe speed, how much fuel it is using, and what the condition of its cargo is. For an automated home, it's the intelligence to understand when something dangerous is happening and taking actions to help prevent it from getting worse.

When it comes to architecting for scale, edge computing is different. The rules for how edge services are built are different, the way they scale is different, and the way they utilize infrastructure is different. Let's take a closer look at edge computing to see how it compares to traditional computing in the cloud and how we need to handle it differently from a scaling standpoint.

Edge Computing Today

These are all great uses of edge computing, but most of these examples are mostly outside of our everyday experiences so far. We don't yet see automated drones flying overhead, nor do we see the impact of micro weather reports on farming.

But significant, important uses of edge computing do exist today, and more are becoming practical every day. You don't need to look too far, or too far into the future, in order to see extensive use of edge computing in action:

- Go to your local grocery store. The scanner is gathering data for the Point of Sale machine to determine how much you owe before sending the results to the cloud.

- Look at your local FedEx agent. They are using a scanner to keep track of your package, so you know where it is at all times and when it is arriving.

- Or look at yourself. You click that button on the application for your favorite coffee shop and expect your coffee to be waiting for you when you arrive.

In all these cases, you are using an edge application and are seeing edge computation.

Even closer to home, do you read your email in a smart web client in your web browser? Yep, that's edge computing as well. The email application has both a server component and an edge component. The edge component is running in your browser. It's running close to you, the user, in order to give you a better user experience.

Yes, that's edge computing as well.

All of these are edge applications. All of them are making use of edge software running in edge devices. The details are different, but the fundamental structure of the application is the same. All of these are examples of edge computing.

Why We Care

Why do we care what is edge computing and what is not? Because patterns for building, operating, and *scaling* edge applications are different than the patterns for building, operating, and scaling cloud-based and server-side applications. The requirements for scaling an edge application or service are very different from the requirements for scaling a cloud application or service. The requirements for keeping an edge application or service operating are also different from the requirements for keeping a cloud application or service operating.

Scaling and availability are both impacted by the type of computation used, whether the computation occurs at the edge or in the cloud.

What Should Be in the Edge Versus the Cloud?

If scaling an application or service and keeping it highly available are impacted by whether or not a service is on the edge, how should we decide whether a piece of computation should be in the edge or in the cloud?

Or put another way, what exactly makes the edge the edge?

To answer this question, let's go back to the purpose of edge computing. The purpose of edge computing is to put time-sensitive operations closer to where they are needed. This means:

- It's about controlling the operation of the drone to keep it flying safely in all conditions and circumstances.
- It's about keeping your browser email application responsive, so when you click a button the application responds immediately.
- It's about keeping home safety systems working even if the connection to the internet (and hence the cloud) isn't currently reliable.
- It's about keeping your mobile application interacting with you in a timely and responsive manner.

This is opposed to the centralized computation that is typical in normal cloud computing. This centralized computation is where data collection and analysis can be done. It's where order processing occurs. It's where communications with other people and systems happens.

Large computing application architecture is all about putting computation where is should be to keep it operating efficiently. This is the key to successful edge computing: putting the computation where it should be to be effective, not necessarily where it is most convenient for developers and operators.

What should be in the edge?

Edge computing is all about putting computation where it should be to operate efficiently and effectively, as opposed to where it is convenient for it to be developed and operated.

Why is this so? Because putting computation out into the edge is harder and riskier than keeping it all together in the cloud. Building and maintaining edge software is more difficult than building and maintaining server-side cloud software.

So when we put computation at the edge, we should do it for good reasons.

How Do We Decide? The Driverless Car

So how do we decide whether to put some computation in the cloud or at the edge? To demonstrate, let's look at an example where both cloud and edge computing are necessary for the application to be successful. It's also an example that is getting lots of attention today and requires a significant amount of both edge and cloud-based computation: the driverless car.

A driverless car is a unique beast. Building and operating a car that can operate independently of a driver requires a significant amount of software and a significant amount of computation. It's state of the art in artificial intelligence and data processing.

Let's take a look at what makes up a driverless car.

A driverless car has lots of sensors and lots of controls. It has sensors to detect where obstacles might be located and where the road is located. It's got cameras to detect whether that blob in front of you is (a) the car you are following, (b) a human crossing the street, or (c) a "road closed" barrier. *Or is it a ball rolling across the street that just might be chased by a small child?* Detecting, determining, understanding, and reacting to each of these possibilities is critical for the car to process in order to make the car safe.

A driverless car also has controls that make the car perform. Of course, it has controls for steering, controls for braking, and controls for applying power. But it also has controls and sensors for monitoring the health of the car itself. Is the motor operating efficiently? Do we have sufficient gasoline in our tank? Is our oil pressure acceptable? Is the passenger compartment cool enough? Should we deploy an airbag right now?

All of this requires computation. Some of this computation has to occur in the car itself, but some of it can occur in the cloud. Which is which? Some things are natural to perform in the car, and for some of that it is, in fact, *mandatory* that it occurs *in the car itself*. Examples of computation that *must* occur in the car itself are:

Image recognition
- Is that a person or another car near me?

Threat detection
- Is that person running in front of me, or is that car in front of me applying its brakes?

Road management
- Where is the edge of the road? Is that a stop sign in front of me?

Collision control
- Do I need to quickly brake and swerve right to avoid a crash?

All of these are time-sensitive calculations that must occur, and in a timely fashion. This processing cannot go offline due to a bad internet connection. It cannot be delayed because a cloud server is busy processing other requests. All of this must occur automatically and immediately and occur every single time on time. It must always be available.

This is computation that must occur in the car itself. This is edge computing for the driverless car.

But there are other calculations that the driverless car needs that can and should occur in the cloud. Examples of computations that can occur in the cloud are:

Driving directions
How do I get from point A to point B? What's the optimal route?

Road conditions
Is there road construction ahead? What about a detour or changed route?

Traffic
Is there traffic on this route that makes taking another route preferable?

Car efficiency
Can we tune a setting in the car to make it operate more efficiently and, perhaps, safe on fuel or emissions?

Car maintenance
Are we running low on gas? Where is the nearest gas station? Do we need maintenance? Where is the nearest maintenance facility?

Fleet, car sharing, and usage management

> Who is using which car? Are we making effective use of our fleet resources? Can we optimize our use of cars to provide better service to our customers? Think about implementing Uber with driverless cars.

All of these things are examples of computations that are important for the operation of the car but are not as time sensitive as the previous list. These items are computations that can, and in fact should, occur in the cloud. These computations typically need access to centralized data, such as maps and traffic information. This information is easier to access in the cloud. Fleet management requires coordinating with other vehicles and other centralized systems. These services need the capabilities available in the cloud that are not easily available in the car itself.

But even more importantly, these computations are not as time sensitive as the edge computation needs are. Determining how to avoid traffic is not as real time as determining whether the person running in front of the car requires you to swerve to avoid them. The performance needs are not the same, and therefore these computations can occur in the cloud.

Software in the cloud is easier to develop, manage, and operate. Cloud software can easily coordinate with other cloud software and can better utilize centralized data and systems.

Software on the edge can respond faster and more reliably to emergent situations. It is more responsive and more adaptable to the particular situation. In addition, software on the edge can provide a higher level of data security given the ability to increase localization of the data and reduce the dependence on centralized data.

Edge Scaling Isn't the Same as Cloud Scaling

Responsiveness and ease of management aren't the only distinctions between software at the edge and software in the cloud. Building software to scale is different in the edge than it is in the cloud. Edge software scales *horizontally*, because adding new users means adding new instances. Cloud software scales *vertically*, because adding new users means the existing software must handle more requests and must scale more.

Edge scaling is all about instance management. How do I upgrade so many instances of my software? How do I monitor how all those instances are performing? Cloud scaling is all about resource management. Do I have the resources it takes to run my software at the required scale?

For software that runs in the edge:

- Edge software typically runs thousands and millions of instances of the software.
- Edge software runs in a huge number of geographically distinct areas, often one instance per location across millions of locations.
- Each instance of edge software typically is doing only one thing at a time, or managing one device or activity.

For software that runs in the cloud:

- Cloud software typically runs substantially fewer instances than edge software. Yes, cloud software may run on tens or hundreds or thousands of servers and instances, but the number of instances is substantially lower than the number of edge instances.
- Cloud software typically runs in a single location or a small handful of locations. Cloud software runs in server farms.
- Each instance of cloud software typically is responsible for managing thousands of distinct tasks, sometimes simultaneously, in order to handle many different user needs.

These differences result in wildly different scaling requirements. As the total application load increases over time, how each system responds to the different scaling needs is different.

For cloud software, the software must scale as the number of simultaneous users increases. The more the software is used, the more instances that must run. You must design and build the software so that more instances can be brought online quickly to meet higher scaling needs, and resource needs and resource allocation must keep scaling in mind in order for the software to keep up with demand and not buckle under the load. For the cloud, load scales upward as usage increases.

For edge software, however, each edge device typically handles a single user and single set of requests. As demand for the software increases, additional independent instances of the edge software are made available, but each individual instance is autonomous and is unaware of other instances. Hence, the load on the edge software is flat even as the number of users of the application increases. The software is not aware of the need to scale.

However, the absolute number of instances required to operate the software for all users grows linearly based on the number of users of the software for edge computing. If you add one million new self-driving cars, you add one million new instances of the software. Each instance of the software still manages only one car, but the number of instances grows considerably. For cloud software, the number of required instances does grow based on the number of users, but not nearly at the same rate. If you add one million new users to a cloud-based application, you might need to add a few tens or hundreds of servers, but definitely not millions.

What does this all mean? For cloud software, resource management becomes the concern. Making sure sufficient resources are available to operate the software at the required scale is your biggest concern in scaling. For edge software, instance management becomes the concern. Managing, operating, upgrading, and monitoring a huge number of instances of the software becomes the biggest concern in scaling.

Criteria for Using Edge Versus Cloud

If it matters whether a service runs on the edge or in the cloud, what criteria should be used to determine which should be used for a particular service or application?

Here is a specific set of recommended criteria for making that determination:

Criteria	Edge versus cloud
Computation is timing specific, or highly sensitive to delays	Edge
You require highly responsive software	Edge
Need a significant amount of compute resources	Cloud
Use of computation is bursty or unpredictable	Cloud
Highly sensitive to network connectivity issues	Edge
Need access to global data and less individualized data (such as traffic patterns)	Cloud
All other situations	Cloud

Why use the cloud for every other situation rather than use the edge? There are multiple reasons, some of which were hinted at earlier. But specifically, here are several reasons why cloud-based services are preferred over edge-based services when possible:

- Edge services are harder to manage and harder to upgrade.

- Edge has various unique provisioning issues. You may have to deal with edge hardware that has multiple versions and hence different capabilities.

- The edge has software version management issues. It's very easy to have different edge devices running different versions of the service software.

- Edge software is harder to monitor and manage due to its highly distributed nature.

Eight Keys to Success in the Edge

We've seen that managing edge software can be more challenging, especially in a highly scaled application. We've also seen why utilizing edge software can be critical for an application. Given this, how can we be successful in using edge computing effectively in our high-scale applications? There are eight keys to being successful in building edge computing into your application. They are all simple but very valuable pieces of advice for success in utilizing edge computing.

#1: Be Smart About What Goes on the Edge

This is a continuation of what was said earlier in this chapter. You must make an *active* decision about whether to use the edge or the cloud for your computation and storage needs.

Remember what the edge is good for and remember what the cloud is good for. And remember the disadvantages the edge has over the cloud. When in doubt, use the cloud. Only use the edge for computation that is best optimized for the edge.

#2: Don't Ignore DevOps Principles in the Edge

It's easy to discount DevOps principles when thinking about edge computing. You will often hear comments like "Edge computing is highly specialized computing" and "New processes and procedures are needed for the edge." These are common messages.

But remember what DevOps is about. DevOps is about:

- Ownership and accountability
- Distributed decision making
- People, processes, and tools (most important)

The processes used in edge computing may change, and the tools you utilize may be different. But there will still be processes and there will still be tools. And the people involved are the same.

DevOps works well even in the edge.

#3: Nail a Highly Distributed Deployment Strategy

Often when we are building an application, we don't think enough about how we will deploy it in production using a highly automated and highly reliable procedure. Instead, we make statements like "we can fix this later." But while automated and repeatable deployments are critical for all applications, they are significantly more important for edge applications. This is true because of the remote nature of edge applications and the huge number of nodes involved.

Without a reliable, highly automated deployment process, your edge-based applications will suffer and fail.

#4: Reduce Versioning as Much as Possible

Deployments at the edge are hard, so reduce the quantity of deployments you need to make for edge applications.

Deploy *less* often.

This goes against the traditional motto of DevOps and Agile application development processes. Why does that make sense?

DevOps and Agile processes utilize CI/CD (continuous integration, continuous deployment) principles. These principles encourage making extensive use of more numerous and smaller deployments. This advice is great for cloud-based and server-based software. But for edge software, versioning becomes an issue. Automation of update processes is critical. The scale of the nodes involved in the upgrade process is huge. The demands of a deployment process are much greater in an edge application than they are in a cloud application. As such, there is value in reducing the number of deployments to reduce the amount of versioning.

There is a fine line here, though. You could reduce your deployments too much and therefore make the size and complexity of each upgrade much greater, increasing the risk of a deployment failure. So use this piece of advice carefully. Reduce versioning as much as possible, *and no more*. Continuous deployment is still a useful strategy, and rapid deployments still have their value. Just balance the effectiveness of this strategy against its increased cost in an edge-based environment.

#5: Reduce Per Node Provisioning and Configuration Options

Given the sheer number of nodes involved in a large edge deployment, it is hard to manage the software for these edge devices unless they are all running the same hardware and hardware version. It is hard to manage the software for these edge devices unless they are running the same software configuration and options. The more diversity in hardware/software settings within the constellation of nodes, the harder it is to manage all these nodes effectively. It's harder to manage, monitor, and upgrade. All aspects of scaling an edge application become more complicated when more provisioning and configuration options are available.

If every remote temperature probe is running on the same hardware, it's easier to build and manage the software. If you have twenty different versions of the temperature probe hardware, or different versions built by different manufacturers, managing all those differences becomes much more complicated; it makes the edge software harder to operate and increases the likelihood of encountering problems.

Of course, it isn't always possible to reduce the provisioning and configuration options. The best example is mobile applications. Mobile applications are edge applications that have to run on a large number of varied hardware/software configurations. This isn't your choice; it's your customer's choice. Having a large number of varied software and hardware configurations is a challenge for all mobile application developers. This problem actually proves my point. Reducing the number of variables makes managing the software much easier. Sometimes this is not possible, but when it is, do it.

#6: Scaling Is an Edge Issue, Not Just a Cloud Issue

Backend cloud scaling is about how much each node can handle and the resource requirements to handle that load. Edge scaling is about how many nodes you can handle.

They are both scaling issues.

Node management is much harder for the edge, and understanding and recognizing that there is a scaling issue with edge software, and how to manage it, is important for building a highly scaled, highly available application.

#7: Nail Monitoring and Analytics

More nodes and distributed nodes mean that understanding how each node is performing at any given time is important. But this is hard to do without good analytics. Edge system management needs a continuous view into the health of every node in a highly scaled system.

Also, high-level reports containing analytics of edge node health tend to be viewed at higher levels within your organization. How an individual server in the cloud or your data center is performing is not of importance to upper management in a typical corporation. But understanding how many automated drones are behaving well versus poorly is considered a higher level of visible importance within most corporations.

#8: The Edge Is Not Magic

Edge computing is not new; it's not "special." We've been doing edge computing for years; we've just called it something else. We might have called it a "browser application" or a "mobile application" or a "Point of Sale" device. But it's all just edge computing.

The edge is not a new form of computing. The edge is, however, a new way to categorize and label an existing class of computation.

This new categorization and labeling is good and encouraging for the future of edge computing, however. It means that in the future there will be *better* edge-focused tooling. There will be services that will be *tailored* for the edge. We are already seeing some of this occur in cloud providers such as AWS that are offering edge- and IoT-focused services.

But *existing* tooling today, non-edge-specific tooling, is still appropriate and useful for building and managing edge services and applications. The edge is not magic.

Edge Computing Overall

These are the eight keys to being successful in building edge computing into your application. Together, they are a simple but very valuable strategy for success in the edge.

It's important to understand what types of applications are best built in the edge and which are best built in the cloud. It's important to understand the impact on scaling an application when it's in the edge versus when it's in the cloud.

It's all about understanding and managing our modern applications and their components, whether they are cloud or edge components.

CHAPTER 20

Geographic Impact on Using the Cloud

This chapter is a departure from other chapters in this book. It's a look at my personal experiences traveling the globe and observing how differences in cultures impact how different areas accept and adopt the cloud and cloud capabilities.

In my current job, I've had the privilege to tour the world talking to companies about the cloud. In these travels, I've noticed that how the cloud is utilized and how it impacts company culture varies based on what part of the world you are in. Much of this is due to country and region cultural differences working their way into corporate culture. If you are working in a multinational corporation and working on cloud adoption, you may find these differences intriguing.

I've specifically noticed trends that vary between Europe, the United States, southeastern Asia, and Australia and New Zealand. Based on my travels, I've identified five specific areas where geographic diversity impacts cloud adoption.

Cloud Matters Everywhere, But at Different Levels

Interest in various ways organizations can leverage the cloud is a universal truth across industries and the world. However, the level and maturity of cloud adoption varies by geography. I talked about cloud maturity in "Six Levels of Cloud Maturity" on page 146, but that focused on corporate culture. What I identified in my travels is that there is a geographic divergence in how the cloud is adopted.

For example, companies based in Australia and New Zealand tend to be faster adopters of cloud technologies than their counterparts in other parts of the world. They hunger for information about what they can do to leverage the cloud to make their businesses better. They proactively look at early technology and want to learn how it might impact and help grow their business.

Conversely, in Germany and other areas of the DACH region,[1] it is the exact opposite. Companies in this region are more safety conscious and want to fully understand the impact of a technology before moving forward with it. When confronted with a piece of technology, their response is frequently, "How is this better than what I already have, and what problems might it cause?" This is a more conservative approach to technology.

Neither way is right or wrong, but they are distinct and unique ways to look at cloud adoption.

Replacement Mentality Impacts How You Adopt Cloud

I noticed a significant difference in how different parts of the world approach fixing and resolving problems across their technology architecture.

To understand this, we need to look at some history, starting back at the beginning of the Industrial Revolution. Historically in Europe and North America, most products that were needed by an industrialized nation were produced locally or at least were readily available along very strong trade routes. As such, it was easy to get equipment, and when equipment broke down, it was easy to get spare parts for that equipment. This created a "replacement mentality" where broken items were easily repaired and replaced and never thought of again. Things broke, but the problems that arose were easily overcome, and the solutions to problems were permanent solutions.

In more remote areas, such as New Zealand, this was not the case. New Zealand is very isolated and had extremely long and thin trade routes. It would historically take six months for products to ship to New Zealand, so replacement parts were hard to come by. If a tractor on a farm broke down, waiting six months for a replacement part meant you lost the entire planting season. As such, companies and individuals had to become quite ingenious in figuring out how to fix broken equipment on their own with only the things they had on hand. Quick and temporary fixes were common, and equipment was held together just well enough to complete the job.

In New Zealand, they even have an expression representing this tendency. That expression is "number 8 wire mentality." It comes from the size of wire that was commonly available in remote areas of New Zealand and commonly used to rig temporary fixes to machinery. The phrase "number 8 wire mentality" is still used today to describe the Kiwi strategy of using whatever scrap materials are on hand to solve a problem.

This difference in approach between well-connected countries and less-connected countries even impacts the current mindsets of companies in these countries today. In

---

1 The DACH region is the countries of Germany, Austria, and Switzerland.

Europe, there is a tendency to fix things using solid, well-defined processes and procedures using well-tested and "approved" methods. This includes software and how they leverage the cloud. In the United States, the tendency follows a more of a replacement mentality. If something breaks, replace it with something that works and move on. Don't sit around worrying about it.

In New Zealand and Australia, however, things are different. In these countries, there is a tendency to fix things using whatever is on hand and to fix things only to the level that is absolutely required to solve the immediate problem. Newer, faster, ingenious techniques that get the job done are prioritized over solid or traditional processes and procedures.

This difference in mentality impacts how cloud vendors should talk to customers in these different locales. New Zealand and Australia eagerly adopted the cloud and newer cloud technologies because it was a new tool in their tool belt to help them fix their problems. In the United States, the cloud was a new and improved way of doing business and was also eagerly adopted.

In Europe, however, the cloud is seen as a new way of doing things that may or may not be better than the current way of doing things. A wait-and-see approach is more often adopted, and the cloud is used only when it is seen to solve a specific, measurable problem.

Which Cloud Is Most Important?

In the United States, Amazon Web Services (AWS) is clearly the favored cloud provider by all measures, but in recent years, questions about Microsoft Azure have been starting to pick up some steam. The same is true in Australia and New Zealand, where it seems that AWS is much more ingrained, and Microsoft Azure has not yet made significant headway into the mindset of the market.

However, in Europe and Great Britain, while AWS is still popular, Microsoft Azure is a part of almost every conversation I have with companies. It is the preferred cloud technology of most people I've talked to.

In all regions, there are a few companies in select industries that have what I call an "allergy to AWS." This includes many retail or ecommerce companies that consider Amazon to be a competitor. This allergy discourages these companies from using AWS, and instead they focus on Microsoft Azure and Google Cloud Platform (GCP). This impact is strongest in the United States and in Europe, and seemingly less pervasive in Asia.

GCP rarely comes up in enterprise customer discussions, but when it does it's mostly in companies with an "allergy to AWS." IBM Cloud comes up in Europe, especially in the DACH region, but rarely elsewhere.

Important Technologies Differ

In each geography, there are different cloud technologies that have a different level of importance. Some of the differences include:

Private cloud

While private cloud was a popular buzzword early in the history of the cloud, it has become less significant and less pervasive across most of the world...except in Germany and other countries in the DACH region. In these countries, there is a strong focus on private cloud. This drive is primarily due to government, business, and consumer security and privacy concerns that companies in this region still see as a problem with the public cloud today. These concerns limit the ability of companies in this region to move to the public cloud, and hence putting private cloud capabilities in their own data centers becomes the next best option.

Containerization

While containerization is popular throughout the world, there is a specific increased interest in Great Britain and throughout continental Europe. In Great Britain and parts of Europe, it's seen as a way to leverage Microsoft and Linux technologies together more easily.

Security

Cloud security is important to everyone. However, this was generally considered a known and solvable issue in most places I visited. In Germany, however, it was considered the primary issue inhibiting public cloud adoption.

DevOps and CI/CD

People were eager to discuss these topics in the United States, Australia, New Zealand, Great Britain, and the Netherlands. In DACH, these topics were less pervasive—not surprisingly, given their approach to cloud adoption.

Data Sovereignty Is Universal

There was one aspect of cloud computing that was universally important—data sovereignty. Data sovereignty is the desire to keep customer data located in the same country where the data is created and consumed.

There is simultaneously a strong need to:

Keep data local for performance reasons

For actively accessed data, latency is a major concern, especially in the Asia Pacific region, where latencies to other countries are traditionally higher. Having data geographically closer improves the customer experience significantly. This causes a focus in Asia Pacific to have data located in Asia Pacific cloud regions.

Have control over their data locally

Keeping control of all data is also of concern. Newly enacted laws and upcoming law changes are requiring companies to look at how data is stored and where it is stored. Increasingly, storing data out of region is considered a security and privacy issue.

Keep data out of the United States

This is a corollary to having data controlled locally. Even if data can't be kept within a country's boundaries, there is a growing need to keep the data out of the United States specifically. There is growing concern among international organizations that data stored within the United States is not private and not safe from prying eyes within the US government. This is a concern for backup and disaster recovery scenarios as well as for live and active data. These concerns were universal in all discussions in all countries outside of the United States.

My Take

It's important to understand that the culture around cloud adoption is something that varies not just from one company to another but from one country to another. There are real and significant differences in how the cloud is seen and utilized in different parts of the world, and understanding these differences is important for people working across these geographic boundaries.

PART VI

Conclusion

Architecting for scale is about more than just handling large numbers of users.

CHAPTER 21

Putting It All Together

We have covered a lot of material in a lot of different topics in this book that, when taken together, is designed to help you scale your applications. We focused on five tenets:

- Tenet #1—Availability: Maintaining Availability in Modern Applications
- Tenet #2—Modern Application Architecture: Using Services
- Tenet #3—Organization: Scaling Your Organization for Modern Applications
- Tenet #4—Risk: Risk Management for Modern Applications
- Tenet #5—Cloud: Utilizing the Cloud

Tenet #1—Availability

Availability is the ability of your application to perform the tasks it is capable of doing. This differs from reliability, which is the ability of your application to not make mistakes. A system that adds 2 + 3 and returns 6 has poor reliability. A system that adds 2 + 3 and never returns a result has poor availability. Poor availability is caused by many things, including the following:

- Resource exhaustion
- Unplanned load-based changes
- Increased number of moving parts
- Outside dependencies
- Technical debt

Application availability is often the first casualty as an application tries to scale beyond its capabilities. We learned what availability was about, how to measure it, and how to apply tools for improving availability in highly scaled applications, even in light of continuously increasing scaling needs.

Tenet #2—Architecture

A service is a distinct enclosed system that provides business functionality in support of building one or more larger products. Services provide an application architecture pattern that facilitates building systems in a manner that promotes improved system and development team scalability.

When building highly scaled applications, services provide the ability to make improved scaling decisions, accommodate improved team focus and control, reduce complexity at the local level, and improve testing and deployment capabilities.

We provided tools and suggestions for how to build high availability into your application at the service level and reduce the effect of service failures on your application and its users.

Tenet #3—Organization

Scaling impacts your organization, not just your application. We looked at the Single Team Owned Service Architecture paradigm, or STOSA. This provides a model for scaling your development organization as your application scales, making it possible for a larger number of engineers to effectively work on a single application without sacrificing application scalability or availability. This involves defining what it means to be a service owner and organizing your application around these principles.

We talked about using tools for managing service dependencies to maintain application quality even during times of hypergrowth, including internal SLAs and service tiers.

Tenet #4—Risk

You cannot possibly manage the risk in your system if you cannot identify the risk in your system. This is the critical lesson from Tenet #4—Risk Management for Modern Applications. Understanding your risk is the first and most important step in operating a highly available, highly scalable application.

After you understand your risk, you must manage that risk. Although removing risk is always desirable, often the cost of doing so is unacceptably high, both from an actual cost standpoint and from the standpoint of the opportunity cost to your application. You certainly have more important, more customer-focused things to do that are better for your customers, your company, and your bottom line than to remove every ounce of risk you know from your application.

Managing risk involves evaluating two values with every risk: the risk's *likelihood* and the risk's *severity*. Generally, severity is the cost to you if a risk happens, whereas likelihood is the chance of the risk happening. A risk that can cause a very serious problem in your application but is improbable might not be one that you want to try removing. Similarly, a risk that is highly likely to happen but would have very little impact on your application is probably not a risk you will need to prioritize removing. But a risk that is somewhat likely to happen and can cause a reasonably serious problem might in fact be the most important risk for you to work on resolving.

We introduced a tool called the *risk matrix*, which can be quite effective in helping you manage the risks of your application and determine which risks need to be mitigated or removed.

We discussed techniques for mitigating risk, techniques for validating mitigation action plans, and techniques for building applications with reduced risk.

Tenet #5—Cloud

Finally, we looked at the cloud and how you can use it to build highly scaled applications.

We looked at how the cloud has changed the way we think about computing and the way we think about building applications. We discussed building geographic and network topographical diversity into your application using the cloud, and how to avoid pitfalls where you believe your application is geographically and network-topologically diverse when in fact it might have built-in dependencies that increase your risk of problems.

We addressed the use of managed infrastructure and how you can utilize it in highly scaled applications. We covered how cloud-based resources are allocated, and the role you need to play in ensuring that your applications have the cloud resources they need to keep operating.

We then discussed compute options available to you when using the cloud. We looked at AWS Lambda, and the revolutionary future in scalable development it enables.

Architecting for Scale

Architecting an application for scalability is more than building an application that handles lots of users at the same time. There are many things involved in making an application scalable:

- It must handle a large and growing number of customers; a large and growing quantity of data used by your customers; and a growing complexity in what your customers want to accomplish with your application.

- You need to add more developers to work on your application as your company's needs expand, and you must do so without sacrificing development speed, efficiency, or application quality.

- Your application must be kept online and functioning, even in light of all of the aforementioned changes and improvements.

These aren't easy problems to solve. The techniques discussed in this book are designed to help you solve these and many more of your application scalability concerns.

In Memoriam
Cherise Watts, my stepdaughter
1981–2019

Index

Internet of Things (IoT), data intake, 197
intuition not matching reality, 30
invalid customer input, failures from, 68

J
joint cloud applications model, 152, 155

K
key-based data partitioning, 54
Kubernetes, 43

L
legal/regulatory requirements
    determining service boundaries, 45
    maturity of compliance in cloud services,
        159
lift-and-shift cloud migration, 150
likelihood vs. severity of risks, 110-114
    high likelihood, high severity risk, 113
    high likelihood, low severity risk, 112
    low likelihook, low severity risk, 111
    low lilelihood, high severity risk, 111
    setting likelihood and severity fields in risk
        matrix, 118
limit SLAs, 99
load time, SLA for, 94
load-based changes, unplanned, 5
localizing data, benefits of, 54

M
maintenance, planned outages for, 8
managed hosting, 161
    comparison to SaaS, 162
    defined, 162
    largest difference between SaaS and, 165
managed infrastructure, 177-184
    structure of cloud-based services, 177-182
        raw resources, 178
        server-based managed resources, 180
        serverless-managed resources, 181
    using managed vs. non-managed resources,
        implications of, 183
metrics
    from cloud server-based managed resour-
        ces, 181
    provided by AWS EC2 instances, 179
micro startups, 158
microservices

acceptance of microservices-based architec-
    tures, 157
    increased complexity with, 136, 138
    industry trend toward, 43
    services and, 44
mitigation of risk, 108, 122-124
    mitigation plans in risk matrix, 119
    used in conjunction with risk matrix, 125
monitoring availability, 20
monitoring in edge computing, 211
monolithic applications vs. service-based, 37-42
moving parts, increased number of, 5
multi-tenant SaaS, 187
    advantages for customers, 163
    advantages for the vendor, 163
    defined, 162
    disadvantages of, 164
    mixing with single-tenant, 165
    vendors providing multiple stacks, 164

N
Netflix, Chaos Monkey, 130
network partition, testing, 130
New Relic monitoring system, 20
nines, the, 7
node, losing in a web service, 25-27
noncritical dependencies, 90

O
online store example, service tiers, 85-87
online T-shirt store example
    likelihood vs. severity of risks, 110-114
        custom fonts, high likelihood and low
            severity risk, 112
        order database, low likelihood and high
            severity risk, 111
        T-shirt photos, high likelihood and high
            severity risk, 113
        Top 10 List, low likelihood and low
            severity risk, 111
operational processes, standardizing on,
    140-141
organizations
    cloud adoption and, 149
    scaling and, 222
organizations, STOSA-based, 74
    advantages of, 75
    hierarchy, 77
    non-STOSA-based organization, 75

building systems with reduced risk, 133-141
    encouraging simplicity, 138
    independence of components, 136-137
    introducing redundancy, 134-136
    security, 138
    self-repairing processes, 139
    standardizing operational processes,
        140-141
    mitigating to keep a system highly available,
        18
risk management, 107-125
    disaster recovery plans, 125
    identifying risk, 107
    identifying, labeling, and prioritizing know
        risks in risk matrix, 114-122
    improving our risk situation, 125
    likelihood vs. severity, 110-114
    likelihood vs. severity of risks
        high likelihood, high severity risk, 113
        high likelihood, low severity risk, 112
        low likelihood, high severity risk, 111
        low likelihood, low severity risk, 111
    mitigation of risk, 108
    recovery plans, 124
    regular reviews of risk matrix, 109
    removing worst offenders, 108
    risk mitigation, 122-124
    summary of important steps, 109
risk matrix, 10, 114-122
    creating, 107, 117-120
        brainstorming the list, 117
        mitigation plan, 119
        risk item details, 119
        setting likelihood and severity fields, 118
        triggered plan, 119
    determining scope of, 116
    example risk entry for a worst offender, 108
    information in example matrix, 114
    maintaining, 120
        regular reviews of risk matrix, 121
    regular reviews of, 109
    sharing with management, 122
    using for planning, 120

S

SaaS (see Software as a Service)
scaling
    always keeping in mind, 17
    architecting for scale, 223

benefits of service-based applications over
    monolithic, 42
in edge applications, 211
in edge vs. cloud applications, 206
in serverless-managed resources, 182
main tenets of, 221-223
    architecture, 222
    availability, 221
    cloud, 223
    organization, 222
    risk, 222
of edge applications, 203
power of FaaS, 195
security
    cloud security concerns in different geo-
        graphic locations, 216
    determining service boundaries, 45
    high-quality, implementing to reduce risk,
        138
    in the cloud, 147
    maturity of cloud security, 159
    not trusting cloud security, 150
    separate team ownership of a service for, 46
selective cloud applications model, 153
self-repair, building into your system, 139
serverless computing, 148, 158
    Functions as a Service (FaaS), 195-200
        advantages and disadvantages of, 198
        example application, event processing,
            196
        example application, Internet of Things
            data intake, 197
        serverless hype and future of FaaS, 199
    lure of, depending too much on the hype,
        151
    serverless-managed resources, 178, 181
        advantages of, 182
servers
    calculating number needed per data center,
        29
    from cloud providers, 177
    independence of, 137
    rebooting, automating process of, 140
    server-based managed resources, 178, 180
        impact of using, 181
    testing server failure, 129
service limits, providing, 69
service ownership (STOSA), 73-79

About the Author

Lee Atchison is the senior director of cloud architecture at New Relic. For the last eight years he has helped design and build a solid service-based product architecture that scaled from startup to high-traffic public enterprise.

Lee has 33 years of industry experience, including seven years as a senior manager at Amazon. At Amazon, he led the creation of the company's first software download store, created AWS Elastic Beanstalk, and managed the migration of Amazon's retail platform from a monolith to a service-based architecture.

Lee has consulted with leading organizations on how to modernize their application architectures and transform their organizations at scale, including optimizing for cloud platforms and service-based architectures, implementing DevOps practices, and designing for high availability.

Lee is an industry expert and is widely published and often quoted in publications such as *InfoWorld*, *ComputerWorld*, *Diginomica*, *IT Brief*, *ProgrammableWeb*, *The New Stack*, *CIOReview*, *DevOps Digest*, and *DZone*. He has been a featured speaker at events across the globe from London to Sydney, Tokyo to Paris, and all over North America.

Colophon

The animal on the cover of *Architecting for Scale* is a textile cone snail (*Conus textile*). It is also known as the "cloth of gold cone" due to the unique yellow-brown and white color pattern of its shell, which usually grows to about three to four inches in length. The textile cone is found in the shallow waters of the Red Sea, off the coasts of Australia and West Africa, and in the tropical regions of the Indian and Pacific Oceans.

Like other members of the genus *Conus*, the textile cone is predatory and feeds on other snails, killing its prey by injecting them with venom from a radula, an appendage that resembles a small needle. The conotoxin used by the textile cone is extremely dangerous and can cause paralysis or death.

Their shells are sometimes sold as trinkets, but textile cones are plentiful, and their population is not threatened or endangered. Many of the animals on O'Reilly covers are endangered; all of them are important to the world.

The cover illustration is by Karen Montgomery, based on a black and white engraving from *Wood's Illustrated Natural History*. The cover fonts are Gilroy Semibold and Guardian Sans. The text font is Adobe Minion Pro; the heading font is Adobe Myriad Condensed; and the code font is Dalton Maag's Ubuntu Mono.